VOLCANOES

VOLCANOES

DAVID PYLE

Oceana

An Oceana Book

This book is published by
Oceana Books
The Old Brewery
6 Blundell Street
London N7 9BH

ISBN 1-86160-232-4

OCEVCO

Project Manager: Rebecca Kingsley
Project Editor: Sarah Harris
Designer: Bruce Low

Typeset in Gill Sans Light
Manufactured in Singapore by Eray Scan Pte Ltd
Printed in Singapore by Star Standard Industries Pte. Ltd.

C O N T E N T S
...

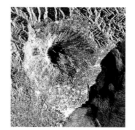

INTRODUCTION

An active volcano is one of the most beautiful and awe-inspiring sights of the natural world. The immense power of even a small eruption makes the largest explosion produced by man seem almost insignificant. The effects of volcanic eruptions can often be seen and felt around the world for months or even years after the event. The aftermath of a large eruption can take many forms, from the beauty of a particularly dazzling sunset, to the brutality of a tidal wave. Almost every generation has experienced the effects of an eruption in some way.

All volcanoes tell us something about the planet we live on, and give us important clues to the part that eruptions play in our ever-changing climate. In the past there have been eruptions on a scale many times larger than anything experienced this century, but even small, little-known volcanoes have their own fascinating history. Further afield, across the solar system, volcanoes play a key role in shaping the surfaces of planets and their moons, and in teaching us more about how the Earth works.

Our very existence depends on volcanoes. Without volcanoes to gush forth water and gas from deep within the Earth, our

250 thousand years of volcanic history preserved in the cliffs of the Santorini caldera.

atmosphere and oceans would not exist, and our planet would be a very different place. Today, tens of millions of people live on and around active volcanoes, relying on them as sources of energy, as well as for fertile soil, hot water and steam. Yet living with volcanoes is not without its dangers. Many thousands of

The Kilauea volcano at Hawaii is one of the most active volcanoes in the world. Here an explosion is caused as a lava flow from the Pu'O'o crater hits the sea.

people have died in volcanic eruptions over the past century, and hundreds of thousands more have suffered the misery of losing their homes to ash and lava. As we come to understand volcanic behaviour, we should be better able to live in harmony with volcanoes, learning which are safe, and which present the greatest risks.

Myths and legends have grown up around volcanoes in many parts of the world. One of the favoured locations for the legendary lost city of Atlantis, for example, is the Greek island volcano of Santorini. This island was completely transformed after a huge eruption about 3,500 years ago. Thick layers of white pumice and ash from this eruption still cover most of the island, like the icing on a cake. On

Small ash plume rising from Etna's summit, May 1992. The cinder cone in the middle was formed during an eruption in the 18th century.

heading into the sea. Finally, in 1886 the veil was used for a third time, when the citizens of Nicolosi were driven by desperation to seek a miracle. The result was the same. The course of the lava was diverted, and the town was saved.

Elsewhere, history has repeated itself with more tragic consequences. At the foot of Nevado del Ruiz, one of many snow-capped volcanic cones in the Andes, nestles the Colombian village of Armero. In February 1845, a small eruption sent cascades of ash and melting snow flooding down the steep valleys that score the volcano's sides. This mixture of ash and snow turned into a boiling mudflow that raced downhill, devastating the Lagunillas valley and destroying everything in its path. Whole villages, themselves built on the remains of a mudflow from a previous eruption, were buried under fresh deposits of mud and ash. Inevitably a new town eventually grew up on top of this latest mud-flat. In an eerie echo of the past, this town, Armero, was destroyed and its 25,000 inhabitants killed when a small but expected eruption sent a mudflow cascading down the same route in 1985.

Etna, eruptions are so frequent that villages on its slopes can expect to be overrun with lava every two or three hundred years. The effects of past eruptions have been deeply etched into the collective memories of villagers, as has an unusual but effective method of damage limitation. The veil belonging to St Agatha, who was martyred in the city of Catania in 250 AD, is believed to hold extraordinary powers. In 252 AD, her veil was carried to the front of a lava flow that was advancing on the city. Almost immediately the lava flow stopped. Centuries later, during another huge eruption in 1669, the city inhabitants turned to the veil for salvation. Again the veil was carried to the lava front, and again the flow changed course,

Oldoinyo Lengai, Tanzania, 1988.

While divine power has been sought in some areas of the world to save inhabitants from the effects of volcanic eruptions, other

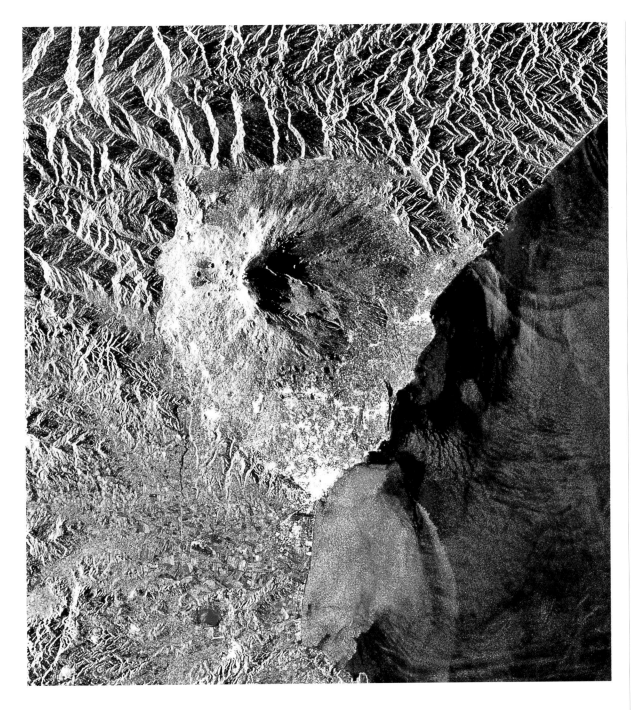

Coloured multi temporal radar image showing Mount Etna. The crater is the dark feature just upper left of centre.

cultures see volcanoes as angry spirits that constantly need to be appeased. This appeasement often took the form of human sacrifice, particularly across South America. Even today, Maasai herders make offerings to the African volcano of Oldoinyo Lengai whenever it erupts, although these take a rather milder form, being offerings of milk.

Today's sacrifices are offered in the name of science, as sensitive instruments to monitor eruptions are placed in the line of fire. This equipment measures the rise and fall of the slumbering volcanoes, listens to the sounds of their quiet stirrings, and follows changes in the makeup and temperature of their fumes. One day such equipment may allow us to anticipate future volcanic eruptions.

CHAPTER ONE

WHAT VOLCANOES ARE

The interior of the Earth is in a perpetual state of turmoil. Although unseen to us on the surface, the sound waves that echo around the Earth after a large earthquake give us many clues as to what is happening beneath our feet. The outer layer of our planet is roughly one hundred kilometres thick, and is relatively cold and stiff. This outer skin is broken up into large fragments, known as tectonic plates, that fit together like the pieces of jigsaw puzzle. More than a dozen of these plates cover the surface of the globe today.

Deeper inside the Earth it is so hot that rocks lose their cohesion, taking on a consistency almost like softened toffee. These rocks creep through the Earth continuously, although at a very slow rate.

Six hundred year old domes of lava, Mono Craters, California, USA.

Lava flows into the sea at 1000-1200 degrees Celsius, Hawaii.

Liquid rock accounts for only a small amount of the material that makes up the interior of our planet, as it can only occur when temperatures exceed the melting point of the rock. Molten rock (melt) is lighter than the solid rocks around it, and, like bubbles of gas in a liquid, sheets and bubbles of melt squeeze their way through the surrounding rocks towards the surface. As the melt rises towards the top of a rigid plate, it has to open up fractures to move upwards. Sometimes these fractures, or dykes, open up all the way to the surface, where they burst out with spectacular results. Usually, though, these fractures feed the molten rock into huge tumbling vats, or chambers, that lie just a few kilometres beneath the surface.

Volcanoes are the pressure valves of the Earth's boiling interior, releasing gas, heat and

Snow covered Mount Fuji, a volcano on the island of Honshu, Japan. At 12,389 feet (3776m), it is the highest in Japan.

molten rock at the surface. Their positions reflect the movement of hot rock inside the earth, as well as the intricate outlines of the tectonic plates. Molten rock, or magma, is the lifeblood of Earth's volcanoes. Without the supply of this molten rock from deep within the planet, there would be no volcanoes.

Most volcanoes form at clearly defined points or lines of weakness in the Earth's plates. Volcanoes can range from the classical conical peaks of Mount Fuji, to huge craters, and from single cones to groups and chains of vents. Magma is not the same from one volcano to another. Rather it is the properties of the molten rock itself that define the shape, size and behaviour of the volcano at the surface.

Magma is a general term for all molten rock before it has reached the Earth's surface, and it is an extraordinary material. Once magma reaches the surface it can erupt as either lava or a mix of ash and pumice. Lava is a stream of liquid rock, while ash or pumice is a violent spray of more-or-less solid rock.

Metre-wide bubbles of gas bursting into a lava pond, Oldoinyo Lengai, Tanzania.

Geothermal steam vent, Roaring Mountain, Yellowstone National Park, USA. About 600,000 years ago a huge eruption emptied a large underground magma chamber. The roof collapsed, forming a giant caldera.

Three main materials are found in magma. The first is the molten rock itself. Inside this molten rock, crystals are frequently formed, and these crystals, of which there are several different kinds, are usually present in magma. Each is identifiable with the naked eye. The final element is gas - usually water or carbon dioxide - in the form of bubbles.

The outer skin of the Earth is rich in the two elements of silicon and oxygen. These same elements are also abundant in most molten rocks. However, not all rocks are the same. Magma that contains relatively small amounts of silicon, such as that found on Iceland or Hawaii, is very fluid. Fluid lavas build up shields that can reach many kilometres from top to bottom. The magma that erupts from these volcanoes as lava is known as basalt. Basalt often forms the familiar rivers of red lava that snake to the sea, or the dancing curtains of red-hot spray that can stretch for kilometres

A cloud of steam issues from the Sakurajima volcano on the Japanese island of Kyushu.

across the landscape. As the amount of silicon in the magma increases, so does the stickiness of the lava, in just the same way as the consistency of a flour and water mixture alters as the proportions change.

As the lavas become more sticky, they flow less easily, and eruption becomes harder. This causes the character of the volcano to change. Sticky lavas build up steep cones or rugged humps that can tower two or three kilometres above their surroundings. One example of a volcano erupting sticky lava is Montserrat, in the Caribbean. Here, lava that arrives at the surface has about twenty percent more silicon in it than lava found on Hawaii. It is also about a million times stickier than Hawaiian lava. Rather than flowing away from the volcano, this lava simply piles up in heaps around the vent to form a dome of lava. Like a squeezed tube of toothpaste, the stack of lava that makes the dome can only grow so big before it starts to fall apart. This

slowly erupting, crumbling type of volcano is particularly dangerous as the eruptions can continue for a long time, and predicting where and when the lava dome will collapse is impossible.

As proof that appearances can be deceptive, some of the least impressive-looking volcanoes are actually formed by the stickiest, and therefore the most dangerous, magmas of all. When magma becomes too sticky to flow easily to the surface as a lava, the pressure builds, and when the eruption finally occurs it is explosive, and often unpredictable.

A volcano that erupts a mixture of ash and lava will generally build up a cone, which is easily recognisable, but those that erupt most violently often leave the most slender clues to their origin. These are the giant caldera volcanoes. A caldera is simply a volcanic cauldron - a large circular hole that marks the position where the rocks of the volcano have collapsed into the emptied magma chamber below. Sometimes, for example in Santorini, these cauldrons can be spectacular, with cliffs rising vertically hundreds of metres from the flooded base of the caldera. Many of the largest calderas are too large to see clearly. The huge lake Toba, the largest lake in Indonesia, is over 100 kilometres long, and 40 kilometres across. This is the site of the largest known eruption of the past hundred thousand years. Cerro Galan, an enormous caldera in Argentina and one of the largest in the world, measures 40 kilometres across and is over 750 metres deep. So large is this caldera, that it was only during the 1970s that images provided by orbiting spacecraft revealed its volcanic origins.

Volcanoes vary in shape and size, and they can also have very different habits and life

Infrared satellite image of the Cerro Galan volcano (upper centre left), Argentina.

expectancies. At one end of the spectrum, the small spatter cones that dot areas of the globe such as the south-western United States and parts of the Azores usually only erupt once. Often these eruptions are tiny, throwing out small quantities of lava to build a small volcanic hill that is perhaps just a few tens of metres tall and hundreds of metres across. Sometimes these eruptions last for a few years, like that at Parícutin in Mexico, which sprung up in a farmer's field in 1943. By the time it finished erupting in 1952, Parícutin had covered a twenty five square kilometre area with lava, and rose over four hundred metres into the air. Other volcanoes spend their whole life erupting more or less continuously. Hawaii's Kilauea volcano has been erupting since the mid 1980's. Sakurajima in southern Japan has been exploding nearly every week since 1955, and

Stromboli in Italy has been blowing gas bubbles since before the time of the Romans.

Most conical volcanoes erupt many times during their lifespan, but live only for a few hundred thousand years. Volcanoes like Vesuvius, or Mount St Helens, are now in their prime of life. Each has had several large-scale eruptions that have thrown out one or two cubic kilometres of molten rock, together with several smaller eruptions. In time - a long time - the movements of the tectonic plates will mean that the path followed by molten rock to the surface will change, and a new volcano will start to form nearby.

Other volcanoes can exist for millions of years. Iceland first started erupting at least 30 million years ago, and is still going strong. However, none of today's volcanoes are more than a few hundred thousand years old, as Iceland's old volcanoes are gradually pushed aside to make way for the new.

Caldera volcanoes might suffer a cataclysmic eruption just a couple of times before dying. These eruptions can be huge; throwing out hundreds or even thousands of cubic kilometres of ash and pumice across the surrounding areas. One eruption of Aso volcano, in Japan, left a deposit that is still tens of metres thick as far away as one hundred kilometres from the volcanic vent. A deposit like this would bury the whole of London and most of southern England.

The extended lifespan of many volcanoes, and the long periods of time that they spend dormant, makes predicting future eruptions very difficult. Three of the most damaging eruptions of the last decades have come from volcanoes which have lain dormant throughout recorded history.

We now recognise more than 1500 active volcanoes around the world. Just over five hundred of these have erupted in the recent past, and together these 500 have been responsible for nearly ten thousand known eruptions over the last ten thousand years. With over fifty volcanoes bursting back into life every year, we are learning new things all the time in our continuing struggle to come to terms with nature's captivating power.

CHAPTER TWO

HISTORICAL EFFECTS OF VOLCANOES

Large eruptions can shake and chill the world. Eruptions such as Krakatau, in 1883, and Pinatubo, in 1991, sent shock waves bouncing around the globe. The sound of the Krakatau eruption was heard over three thousand kilometres away. Huge sea waves, or 'tsunami', swept across much of south-east Asia, while the pressure wave that followed the Krakatau eruption jolted barometers thousands of kilometres distant. Large eruptions can also make the atmosphere hum. After the eruption of Pinatubo, scientists watching sensitive earthquake detection equipment in California picked up a strange signal. This turned out to be the sounds of the atmosphere resonating, much in the same way as a flute resonates with each note played. These effects are tiny, however, compared the effects eruptions can have on the world's weather.

In the late 1700's Benjamin Franklin was the first to notice a connection between eruptions and weather patterns. In 1783, while living in Europe, Franklin noticed that a thin haze reddened and dimmed the glare from the sun throughout the summer. In a

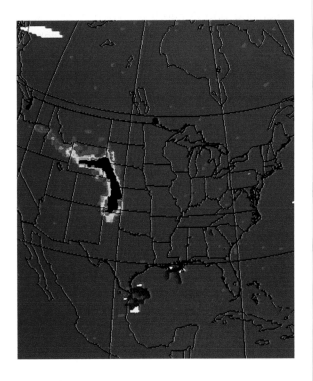

Satellite image of atmospheric sulphur dioxide following the Mount St Helens eruption. Image 1 was taken on 19 May, 1980, a second image (page 21) on 22 May. The black areas indicate the greatest SO2 levels.

flash of inspiration, Franklin suggested that there might be a link between this haze, the harsh winter of 1783-1784 across northern Europe, and the eruption of Laki volcano in Iceland. We now know that there is substance to his theory. Volcanoes can affect the weather patterns around the globe, even up to one or two years after an eruption. Franklin was lucky in that he was in a position to observe the effects of the most damaging eruption in Iceland for many years, and one of the most polluting eruptions of the last millennium.

The largest eruption of the past 200 years occurred in 1815, at Tambora in Indonesia. The following year the weather was so poor in the Northern Hemisphere that it is known as 'the year without a summer'. As the sun's feeble rays struggled to warm the soils, crops failed across Europe and North America, while back in Indonesia, tens of thousands perished through famine. We can see the effects of this eruption in the ice from glaciers across Greenland and Antarctica. When it erupted, Tambora threw out huge quantities of sulphur.

This sulphur was thrown high into the atmosphere, where it changed slowly into tiny droplets of sulphuric acid. These droplets reflected the sun's rays away from the earth, and cooled the surface temperature until they cleared from the air about a year later. Tiny traces of this acid can still be found in the ultra-clean ice at the North and South Poles. During 1815 and 1816, the whole planet was cooled by about one degree, all due to this one eruption.

The effects of past volcanic eruptions on the weather can also be seen in tree rings. Tree growth can be very sensitive to local weather conditions, especially in places such as high mountains, or swampy regions, where the

Small icebergs spilled from the Vatnajokull icecap, Iceland. The grey and black discolouration is debris from volcanic eruptions.

trees are already struggling to grow. Poor weather, such as unseasonable cold spells, leads to narrow rings. Because tree rings can be dated with great accuracy, they help us to put together a picture of weather patterns through the ages. The analysis of tree rings has helped scientists to pick out some of the largest eruptions that have taken place over the past few thousand years.

Within the last two hundred years, both the eruptions of Laki (1783-1784) and Tambora (1815-1816) stand out clearly. The rings also point to 1883 as being a year marked by a large volcanic disturbance. Indeed, this was the year of the great Krakatau eruption, after which there were brilliant sunsets for six months, and the Earth cooled by about half a degree. Although Krakatau is often thought of as the benchmark of a catastrophic eruption, it was by no means the largest. An eruption of this magnitude happens somewhere every hundred years. Looking further back over the records

Comparative Scale of Eruptions

| Tambora, 1815 | Krakatau, 1883 | Vesuvius, AD 79 | El Chichon, 1982 | St. Helens, 1980 |

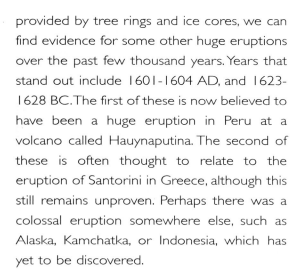

provided by tree rings and ice cores, we can find evidence for some other huge eruptions over the past few thousand years. Years that stand out include 1601-1604 AD, and 1623-1628 BC. The first of these is now believed to have been a huge eruption in Peru at a volcano called Hauynaputina. The second of these is often thought to relate to the eruption of Santorini in Greece, although this still remains unproven. Perhaps there was a colossal eruption somewhere else, such as Alaska, Kamchatka, or Indonesia, which has yet to be discovered.

Written records of the effects of very large eruptions also date back thousands of years. Early Chinese writers took great care to record unusual observations, including changes in the colour of the sun and moon, and the disappearance of stars from the night skies. Both of these features can be due to large eruptions, as volcanic pollution high in the atmosphere allows less light from the sun to reach the Earth's surface. During the peak of a volcanic eruption, the ash-laden skies darken enough to render dim stars invisible, perhaps for months at a time. The ash and other volcanic compounds also soak up light of certain wavelengths and scatter the remaining light, causing the sun and moon to change colour.

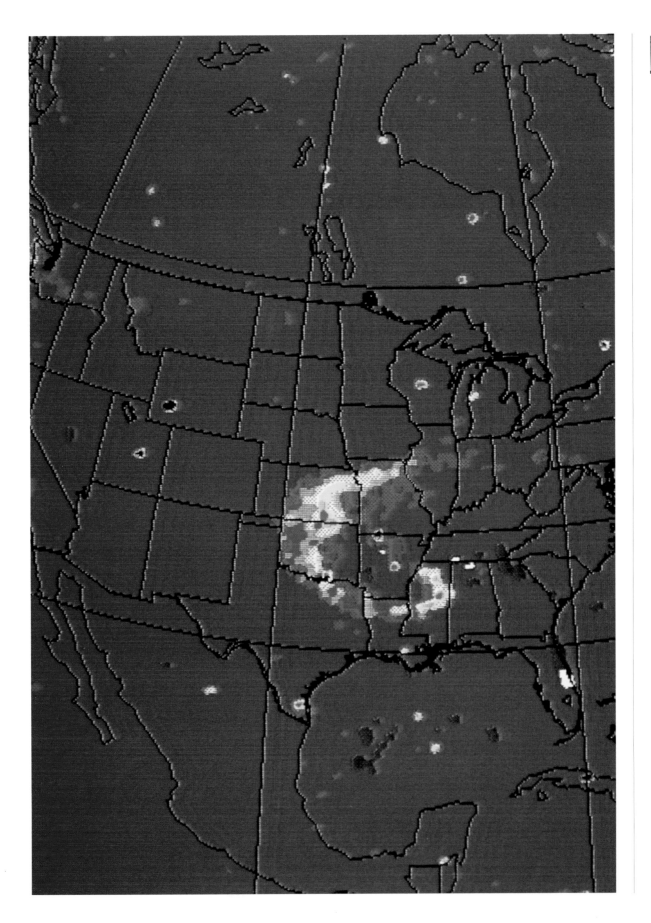

Satellite image of atmospheric sulphur dioxide following the Mount St Helens eruption. This image was taken on 22 May 1980. The black areas indicate the greatest SO2 levels.

CHAPTER THREE

TYPES OF ERUPTION

Volcanoes can erupt in a number of different ways. Some volcanoes only ever erupt in one style, while others switch from one form to another between eruptions, or as an eruption continues. Many of the different sorts of eruption are known by the name of the volcano that typifies the eruption, or where the activity was first seen. However, since the differences between many of eruption types are gradual rather than fixed, it is more useful to think about what happens during a small number of different eruptions than to describe each of the different eruption styles.

LAVA ERUPTIONS

Lava is the most common material produced by volcanoes. Most eruptions of lava take

Plinian column of ash, gas and pulverised rock shooting out from Mount St Helens during the second eruption of 22nd July 1980.

Lava flow, Hawaii.

place away from human sight, as many volcanoes are hidden beneath the sea. In these cases, the eruption can be heard and felt, but not seen. Some of the best examples of lava-producing volcanoes include Hawaii, Iceland and Etna. At each, the process of eruption is similar. Hot molten rock, or magma, rises towards the surface. If the magma is fluid, then bubbles of gas that form in the melt are able to escape. These bubbles of gas form for just the same reason that fizzy drinks bubble when the cap is loosened. The gas stays dissolved in the liquid as long as the pressure is high, but bubbles out when the pressure falls. While these gas bubbles can escape, there is no opportunity for pressure to build up in the plumbing system that the melt moves through to get to the vent. At the surface of the volcano, lava may ooze out gently, or spray out as a vivid fountain of red-hot droplets of rock. Depending on how

Flow of aa lava from Etna approaching the village of Zafferana, May 1992.

fast the lava pours out, the lava may form into long rivers that sweep gently down the valleys around the volcano, or else may build up cinder cones of frozen droplets of magma around the vent. Hawaiian lava is very hot and fluid, so the lava rivers move quickly at perhaps a few metres per second. Like water, lava follows the easiest path downhill, but unlike water it always leaves a trail of hot rock behind.

Etna lava is a little more sticky. Here, flows are thicker and more sluggish, moving at just a few metres per minute. These lavas often make their own channels to flow in, by building up rocky ramparts on either side of the flow. These ramparts can be metres high, and act like walls around the flowing lava. Some volcanoes produce lava millions of times stickier than at Hawaii. This lava barely flows at all, instead building up tall stacks and domes of lava around the vent. On Montserrat, in the Caribbean, these lava domes are two or three hundred metres tall, and grow up at a rate of a few metres per day.

The character of lava can change depending on how fast it is erupted. When lava oozes quietly from a vent, it forms rolling tubes and puddles of smooth-textured 'pahoehoe'. These flows are very gentle, and usually quite thin - perhaps just a few centimetres or tens of centimetres thick. By gradually building up one flow over another, expansive lava fields of pahoehoe can form. Because they are erupted slowly, pahoehoe flows usually do not travel very far from the vent. Instead, they cool off quickly at the front, and a new bud of lava bursts out from nearer the vent.

When lava erupts quickly, it tends to form what is known as aa. This lava is covered in spiny or clinkery blocks, whose size can vary from that of a house brick to an enormous boulder. An aa flow creeps forward behind a snout consisting of rocks and boulders. As it moves, the flow sounds like truck-load after truck-load of stones being dumped across the countryside, tumbling and crashing to the ground. As larger blocks peel off the front of the flow, the red-hot interior is exposed for a moment, quickly darkening as a cool crust forms on the surface. Despite their grey-black appearance, these tumbling blocks are still hot, often causing vegetation to burst into flame spontaneously. Flowing lava is strong enough to carry the weight of these larger boulders on its surface. Indeed, on Etna, it is possible to walk across fresh lava flows, although this is certainly not recommended. The lava is too sticky to fall into, even though it looks like a fluid when it moves.

Thin pahoehoe flows, Oldoinyo, Lengai, Tanzania.,

Old pahoehoe lava flows high on the flanks of Etna.

EXPLOSIVE ERUPTIONS

While many volcanoes erupt lava freely, others have more difficulty because the lava is too sticky. In this case the pressure has to be released in a different way. As sticky lava rises towards the surface, the small bubbles of gas that grow within the liquid are unable to move. Instead, as they grow they build up pressure inside the walls of the conduits which they are rising through. Eventually, the bubbles are so large and so close together that the lava has the consistency of an exceedingly stiff foam. The material then breaks up spontaneously, forming a mixture of lumps of broken rock, pumice and ash in a hot gas. This mixture flows freely, and accelerates towards the surface. If there is a simple conduit open to the surface, the mix of ash and pumice will reach the speed of sound, a few hundred metres per second, by the time it emerges from the crater. This is the start of an explosive eruption. What happens next depends on a number of different factors. As the hot jet of material leaves the vent, it races skywards. As cool air becomes mixed in with the jet, it is transformed into a grey billowing cloud that will punch its way high into the air. The more powerful the jet, the higher the eruption cloud will rise, taking huge blocks of rock and pumice with it.

Occasionally, if the jet runs out of energy before it can mix with air, then fountains of

hot rock and ash can spill back over the volcano as deadly 'pyroclastic flows'. These form in a similar way to a fountain of water. If the water pressure is high, it is easy to make a tall fountain. But eventually, the stream of water slows to a halt, after which it must fall back to Earth. In a similar fashion, volcanic jets can rise a few hundred metres above the volcano before collapsing back as a fountain of hot rock and ash.

Pyroclastic flows can be tremendously violent. They are like avalanches of hot rock, but they move like a liquid. On steep volcanoes, these flows can move at over 100 miles an hour. They are eerily silent, with clouds of ash rising for thousands of feet above them.

Explosive volcanic eruptions can be spectacular affairs. They may start with little or no warning, although usually there are some clues to what is about to happen. Once started, they can be over very quickly, perhaps in a matter of days, or even hours. Often, as in the case of the eruption of Vesuvius that destroyed Pompeii, the eruption changes as time passes.

The AD 79 eruption of Vesuvius started with a rising column of ash and pumice that shot over twenty kilometres into the air. To Pliny, who described the eruption from out at sea, this billowing cloud looked like a Mediterranean Stone Pine. A slender column of ash fed a huge cloud that was blown south and east by the winds. As time passed, the eruption continued, but there were peaks and troughs in the activity. Several times parts of the billowing clouds failed to rise, but instead collapsed to the ground to form pyroclastic flows. These flows would have been terrifying to experience. First the falling stones and rock powder would have made visibility appalling.

Terraces of pyroclastic flows, Mount Pinatubo. Flows several hundred metres thick were emplaced during the peak of the eruption.

Aa flows, just tens of centimetres thick, creeping across the floor of the Oldoinyo Lengai crater.

This was followed by a blast of burning hot air which came rushing through the streets, laden with boulders and more ash. Heaving clouds of ash and forks of lightning would have rumbled threateningly above the blast. From the thick deposits left behind by the eruption, and the extraordinary archaeological remains, we can build up a minute by minute picture of the eruption. The citizens of Pompeii had no chance against these violent flows. Similar flows have taken a huge toll on those living near active volcanoes around the world, killing nearly thirty thousand people in just a few minutes at St Pierre in Martinique in May 1902, and many thousands more elsewhere.

Other explosive eruptions happen when hot magma heats and boils water. These sorts of eruption are known as 'phreatomagmatic' or 'phreatic' explosions, depending on whether fresh magma is erupted or not. The rock from these eruptions is generally blocky and contains few large bubbles, unlike pumice which is usually more bubbly. These steam explosions can happen with little warning, and can be hugely destructive. Lake Taal, in the Philippines, has had many eruptions like this in its short life, each time threatening the lives of the tens of thousands of people who live around its shores.

CHAPTER FOUR

WHERE VOLCANOES
ARE FOUND

As you can see from any map of the world, volcanoes are not spaced randomly across the Earth's surface. Most active volcanoes are collected into great chains that line the edges of some of the continents and criss-cross the floors of the deep oceans. Only a few rare volcanoes stand isolated, rising from the middle of a land mass or ocean basin.

The oceans of the world hide most of the Earth's active volcanoes. These submarine volcanoes together make up a feature called an 'oceanic ridge'. These ridges would be the most impressive mountain chain on Earth if they weren't hidden from view beneath the sea. One ridge runs like a zip down the middle of the Atlantic Ocean, and then divides, heading across the Indian Ocean and

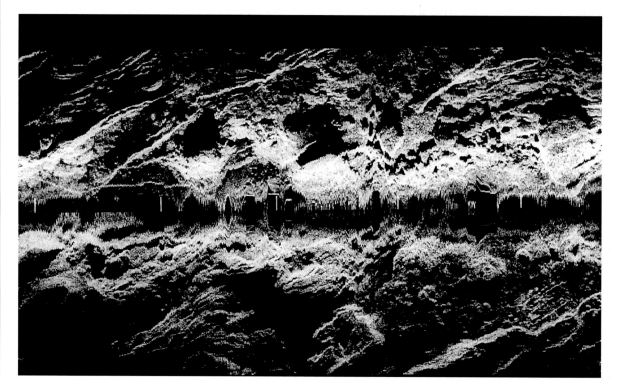

Sonograph of the Reykjanes Ridge, a section of the Mid-Atlantic Ridge south of Iceland.

Deep ocean "smoker" vents in the floor of the Pacific Ocean.

into the Pacific. In places it rises two to three kilometres above the bottom of the sea floor. This ridge marks the place where the Earth's crust is being pulled apart, and where hot molten rock rises from below to fill the space. More than three-quarters of all lava produced in the world forms along one of these ridges. However, the ridges cover such a huge distance, and are so difficult to reach, that none of these eruptions has ever been seen.

In Iceland, the ridge rises above sea-level, and we get a clearer view of how ridges behave. The structure of a ridge is remarkably simple. It is simply a fracture that extends a few kilometres deep into the Earth. All of the volcanoes along the ridge lie close to this fracture. Volcanoes line the fracture system from end to end, spaced anywhere from a few hundred metres to a few kilometres apart. In the centre of the Atlantic Ocean, the Earth's crust pulls apart only very slowly. Volcanoes along this section of the ridge erupt less lava than those elsewhere, and the ridge is shaped into a very deep gully, with steep cliffs on either side of a central valley. Every few hundred kilometres the whole valley is interrupted and moved sideways by another set of huge fractures that cross the ocean floor.

The oceanic ridges of the Pacific Ocean are a little different. Here the Earth's plates are being pulled apart ten times faster than the plates of the Atlantic. More hot rock needs to rise up here to fill the space that is being made, and so the volcanoes of the Pacific 'rise' are younger and more active. In most places, the centre of the ridge is no longer a valley, but a hill.

In a couple of places, these rifts extend into the continents. The best example of this is the great East African rift valley. This runs thousands of kilometres from Ethiopia and Eritrea in the North, to Malawi in the South. This rift is being pulled apart at an incredibly slow rate. This is the reason that the rift is still above sea-level. If the rift had been stretching any faster over its thirty million year history,

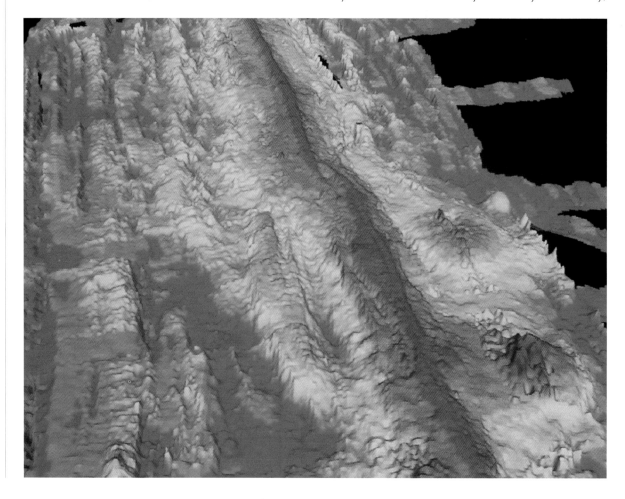

An overlapping spreading centre of the East Pacific Rise.

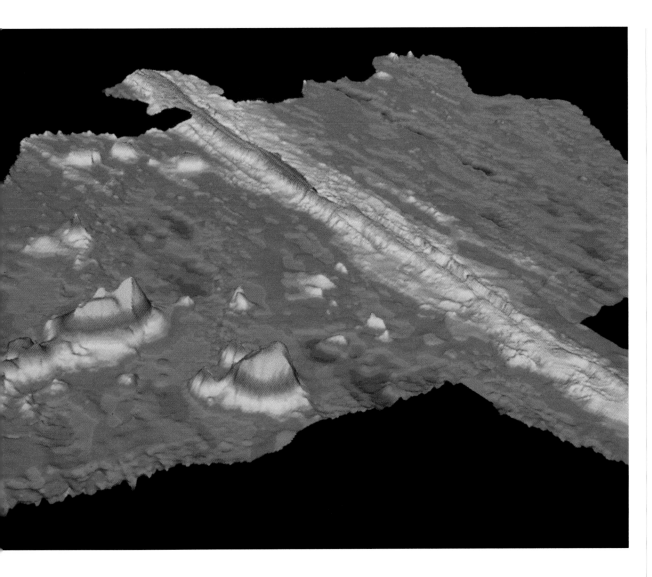

Image of part of the East Pacific Rise. The deepest parts are represented by the dark blue shades, while white represents the shallowest areas.

then it would be a deep ocean by now. All along the rift, huge volcanoes rise from the valley floor. The largest of these are in Ethiopia and Kenya, where caldera volcanoes rise thousands of feet above the surrounding countryside, often having large water-filled craters within their summits.

The most well known chains of volcanoes are those that line the edges of many continents, and which together make up the Pacific 'ring of fire'. These volcanoes, sometimes known as arc volcanoes because of their tendency to lie along gently curved lines, form in regions where one tectonic plate is being destroyed beneath another. Most arc volcanoes lie

between about 100 and 150 kilometres above the plate that is being eroded. These volcanoes also tend to be evenly spaced, lying perhaps a few tens of kilometres apart along the chain. Arc volcanoes include the classical cones of Indonesia, the Philippines and Japan, as well as the chains of huge volcanoes that line the backbone of Central and South America. Smaller chains that include just a handful of volcanoes include those of the Lesser Antilles in the Caribbean; the South Shetland islands of the South Atlantic and the Aegean arc in the Mediterranean.

A few volcanoes have no near neighbours, but instead protrude through the continent or

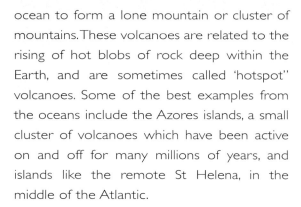

ocean to form a lone mountain or cluster of mountains. These volcanoes are related to the rising of hot blobs of rock deep within the Earth, and are sometimes called 'hotspot" volcanoes. Some of the best examples from the oceans include the Azores islands, a small cluster of volcanoes which have been active on and off for many millions of years, and islands like the remote St Helena, in the middle of the Atlantic.

Hawaii is another example. From a map of the world it looks as though Hawaii is at the end of a long line of volcanoes. This line is not like the other chains that form in rifts or arcs, however, because in the Hawaiian chain the volcanoes are no longer all active. Instead, the further away you move from Hawaii, the older the volcanoes that you will find. This is because the tectonic plate on which Hawaii lies, the Pacific plate, has been moving steadily across the hot spot in the mantle. As the plate has moved, melt has leaked to the surface through a fresh piece of the plate, building another volcano. The line of extinct volcanoes along this chain marks the points where molten rock has erupted over the past 90 million years. The clock is now ticking for Hawaii, as the newest volcano in the chain is starting to grow beneath the sea, at a vent called Loihi.

CHAPTER FIVE

EUROPE

Europe lies on one small corner of a vast tectonic plate that extends beneath Russia, China and south-east Asia. Volcanoes run around the edges of this plate, down the centre of the Atlantic and across parts of the Mediterranean as far as Turkey. A small tear in the plate runs beneath the North Sea and into the Rhine Valley, and this too is lined with volcanoes. Under parts of Central France, hot blobs of molten rock have occasionally risen to the surface, building the volcanoes of the Auvergne and Massif Central.

The story of the plate could have been quite different. Sixty million years ago the North Atlantic was struggling to open. Huge volcanoes formed at the tearing edge, from Rockall and the Faeroe islands down what is now the western side of Scotland. All that remains of these volcanoes are the denuded remnants, standing toothless and impotent. One such volcano forms the island of Rum in Scotland. Rum is one of Britain's youngest volcanoes, and has been extinct for fifty seven million years. It gives us a unique and safe view into the interior of a once active volcano. Rocks now at the surface once filled a chamber teeming with molten rock deep below the ground. The two peaks of Hallival and Askival are made up of white layer upon

black layer of two different minerals, feldspar and olivine. These layers record the arrival of different pulses of molten rock on their way to the surface. Here, the magma cooled a little, dropped some crystals, and then sped to the surface to erupt as showers of red-hot basalt. Now the rock beneath Rum has cooled, and the nearest volcanoes lie hundreds of kilometres away at the mid-Atlantic ridge.

VESUVIUS, ITALY

To find active volcanoes in Europe, we have to travel towards the Mediterranean. Italy has the dubious distinction of hosting some of the most dangerous volcanoes in Europe. Prime among these is Vesuvius. The cramped, bustling city of Naples surrounds and scales the flanks of Vesuvius. Deep within the city are the stark

The interior of a 58 million year old volcano, Rum, Scotland.

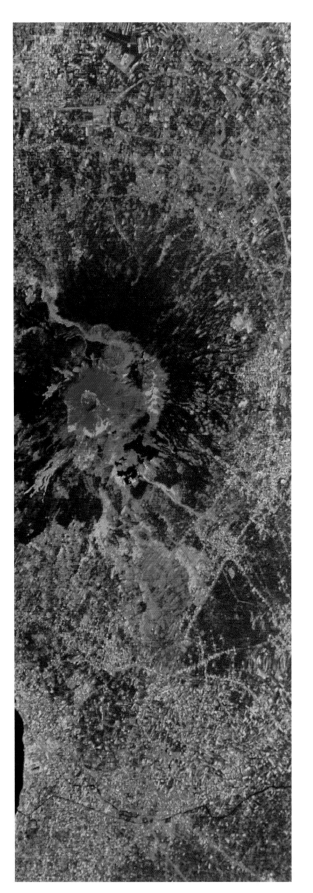

False-colour infrared image of Vesuvius made by an aircraft-mounted Thermal Infrared Multispectral Scanner. The crater is seen just left of centre. Purple areas show relatively recent deposits of volcanic ash, whilst older lava flows show as pink and light blue. Naples is seen as a brown region at the top, while the pinkish dots to the south show the location of Pompeii. Green areas represent vegetation.

remains of the Roman cities of Pompeii and Herculaneum. These once nestled, like the suburbs of Naples, between the sea and the mountain. Vesuvius is an unpredictable and violent volcano. It has a long history of explosive eruptions and, for this volcano, there is no possibility of reform. It will continue to explode.

After the violent eruption of AD 79, which buried Pompeii and Herculaneum under a thick blanket of ash, Vesuvius spent the next thousand years slowly winding down. Occasional eruptions threw a new pall of ash across central Italy, or sent another small lava flow trundling down its flanks. Then, in December 1631, Vesuvius burst back to life. In a scaled-down repeat of the eruption of AD 79, pyroclastic flows hurtled down valleys around the volcano. Thirty centimetres of ash fell on Naples, and thousands died. The speed of the destruction was remarkable, and within a couple of days it was all over.

For the last four hundred years Vesuvius has been cooling off once more. The last eruption was in 1944, and the period since then has been the longest quiet episode since 1631. Perhaps Vesuvius is gearing up again for another large eruption?

ETNA, ITALY

Further South, on the island of Sicily, Etna is one of the world's most prolific volcanoes. Records of Etna's eruptions stretch back for more than two thousand years, and during this time it has rarely been quiet for long. Etna's forte is lava. If it is not gurgling in one of the three chasms that perforate the summit, or gushing from a vent somewhere on the mountainside, there is still every chance that magma is heaving around near the surface.

Artwork showing the explosive eruption of Vesuvius on 24 August 79AD.

Etna is a very mobile mountain. As magma moves around beneath the ground the surface bulges and stretches. Sometimes this bulging shows us where to expect the next eruption to start. It is not unusual to see fissures open up across the mountain, and stretch by a metre or two, before the fissure finally turns into a conduit for hot lava.

In December 1991, Etna's largest eruption for three hundred years started with a fountain of fire bursting high up on its south-eastern side. Fine, dark ash was thrown across villages around the mountain, before the eruption settled down. For the next ten months, torrents of lava gushed out of the new vent. By May 1992, the eruption had reached its most dangerous stage. Lava flows stretched to

May 1992, ash plume rising from Mount Etna.

the outskirts of the village of Zafferana and looked set to sweep through on their way to the sea. High up on the mountain, a team managed to divert the lava flow by blasting a hole in the side of one of the main lava channels. With the flow partially diverted, and the eruption waning, the lava flow stopped advancing and Zafferana was saved. By the time the eruption finished in early 1993, over seven square kilometres of land were covered with a quarter of a cubic kilometre of new lava.

SANTORINI, GREECE

Santorini is a small group of sun-drenched volcanic islands in the Greek Cyclades. A chain of volcanoes, of which Santorini is one, swings across the Aegean sea from Kos and Nisyros, near Turkey, to Milos and Methana. Deep beneath Santorini, the African plate is slowly being destroyed beneath the European plate.

The islands of Santorini used to be part of a single volcanic landmass, and the earliest known volcanism on Santorini was a couple of million years ago. The modern volcano has been active for the last quarter of a million years, and it is highly explosive. Typically, activity switches between repeated, small eruptions that build up large shields of lava, and explosive eruptions that take another bite out of the island.

Today, Santorini is a flooded caldera rimmed by a spectacular set of islands fringed with cliffs. The cliffs rise up to three hundred metres above sea level, and head down as far again below the sea. The prominent layers exposed in the cliffs record past eruptions. At least twelve violent explosions have cut into the heart of the island. Each explosion excavated another deep chunk out of the volcano and cut a new set of cliffs. Santorini's last great eruption was during the Bronze

Lava flow from Etna approaching the outskirts of Zafferana, May 1992. The flow stopped the next day.

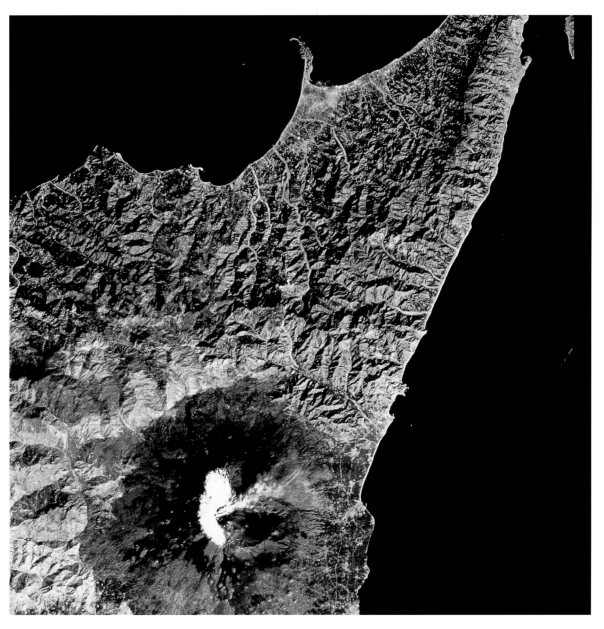

Age, about 3500 years ago. Deposits from this eruption, known as the 'Minoan' eruption, cover much of Santorini with a thick layer of white ash and pumice. In places this layer is over twenty metres thick. The eruption also scattered ash as far away as the Nile delta and across Turkey and the Black Sea. Despite appearances, though, the Minoan eruption was not so very large in geological terms. It was just a little larger than the eruption of Krakatau in 1883.

There is no doubt that the eruption had a major impact across the Aegean. Soon after the eruption started, ash would have begun to fall across the islands south-east from Santorini, and darkness would have descended for a couple of days. The ash plume rose over twenty kilometres into the air, and would have been visible from the Greek mainland, from present day Turkey and North Africa. A small tidal wave washed across much of the eastern Mediterranean. However, beyond Santorini itself, there is

Satellite view of Mount Etna. A plume of smoke and steam may be seen spreading east.

The Kameni Islands, Santorini. These islands of aa lava are the youngest parts of the volcano, and last erupted in 1950.

nothing to suggest that the eruption caused any major destruction or upheaval. Indeed, excavations of the buried town of Akrotiri on Santorini suggest that there was some warning of the impending eruption. No valuables or bodies have been found on Santorini. Perhaps some violent earthquake activity or some small explosions caused the island to be evacuated before the main eruption?

For the last two thousand years a new volcano has been building in the middle of the flooded crater. All of these recent eruptions have been of lava, and they show every sign of continuing on and off for the next few thousand years. If the volcano continues as its long history suggests, another large explosive eruption is not due for another ten or fifteen thousand years. Until then, the most significant threat to the island comes from a small submerged bank, Colombos, that lies out to

sea and away from the main caldera. A small steam and ash explosion there three hundred years ago had devastating effects. So little is known about its past that it is impossible to guess what it might do in the future.

Volcanic deposits at Santorini. Each of the prominent layers were deposited during single explosive eruptions.

CHAPTER SIX

THE AMERICAS

More than half of the volcanoes of the notorious Pacific 'Ring of Fire' line the edges of North and South America, stretching from the volcanic islands of the Aleutians down to the southernmost tip of Patagonia. This ring of fire marks the places where the tectonic plates of the Pacific are being consumed beneath North, Central and South America. It is not a continuous chain of volcanoes, however. There is a brief interruption through California, where the San Andreas fault takes over. Here, the Pacific and North American plates slide past, rather than under, each other. There is another interruption through northern Peru, where the plate that is sliding into the Earth is too shallow to produce

Mineral terrace at a geothermal spring at the Mammoth Hot Springs, Yellowstone National Park, USA. These terraces form at the outflow of deep, geothermal springs.

volcanoes. From top to bottom, this is an incredible region. Alaska and the Aleutians have been responsible for more volcanic eruptions in the last century than most other parts of the world. South America boasts the world's highest volcano, Nevados Ojos del Salado, and the highest and longest volcanic chains. Most of the volcanoes of the region are 'stratocones'. These towering accumulations of lava, ash and pumice reflect long histories of eruptions that are sometimes gentle, sometimes violent. The North American continent has a long history of volcanism, stretching back hundreds of millions of years. Much of this history is preserved in the weathered remnants of once

View of Old Faithful, the world's most famous geyser at Yellowstone National Park.

huge chambers of molten rock. These are now rounded peaks and crags of granite, such as Half Dome and El Capitan of the Yosemite national park. A trail of once-molten rock marks the path of the Columbia River, in the north-western United States. The Columbia River Basalts are ancient 'flood basalts', a thick sequence of lava flows of colossal dimensions. These were mostly erupted between fourteen and sixteen million years ago. Now, they cover over a hundred thousand square kilometres with flows that are each up to one hundred metres thick. So much lava poured out during these eruptions that valleys more than a kilometre deep were filled in and buried by flows. Like most flood basalts, the Columbia River flows were erupted from long fissures. These fissures opened up in the top of the crust, allowing molten rock to spill out. The basalt came from a 'hot spot' in the mantle. This hot rising plume of solid mantle melted as it reached the uppermost parts of the Earth, producing huge quantities of lava at the surface. The trail of this hot spot can be traced as it has made its way across the western United States from the Columbia River Plateau, under the Snake River Plain to Yellowstone where it lies today.

Yellowstone is one of the largest volcanoes in the world. It is old, but still capable of extraordinary feats. In its two and a half million year history, Yellowstone has erupted with colossal violence. In the last of these outbursts, six hundred thousand years ago, about a thousand cubic kilometres of silica-rich 'rhyolitic' pumice was scattered across the western United States. For the past seventy thousand years, Yellowstone has been sleeping. As it slumbers, the volcano rises and falls rhythmically by one or two centimetres per year. 'Old Faithful' and other steam geysers exploit the heat of this sleeping giant,

Landsat image of Mt St Helens volcano, Washington, one of many forming the Cascade Mountains, a range running from northern California through into Canada. The Columbia River forks at the city of Portland (blue). This image was recorded in June 1978, before the devastating eruption of 1980.

which will take many thousands of years more to cool. Yellowstone has already been through three cycles of eruption. Only time will tell whether there is to be a fourth.

MOUNT ST HELENS

Since its eruption in May 1980, Mount St Helens has become the best known of North America's volcanoes. Before 1980, St Helens was just another of the line of snow-clad cones that stretch along the United States' Pacific coast. It was distinguished by its fine, symmetrical shape, in marked contrast with the gnarled peaks of its neighbours Mount Rainier and Mount Adams. In early 1980, St Helens began to show signs of activity. Steam began to pour from fractures near the summit. The snow began to darken as rock fragments became caught up in the violence

of the explosions, and a small crater began to form and deepen near the summit.

During April and early May 1980, the northern side of the volcano began to push out, bulging under the pressure of the molten rock beneath. On the morning of May 18, a moderate earthquake proved to be the final straw. The 'bulge' slid off the volcano's side, triggering a massive explosion. Over the course of the next couple of minutes, a blast of hot ash raced across six hundred square kilometres of prime forest, tossing trees aside like matchsticks. For the rest of the day, a column of ash and pumice rose twenty kilometres above the volcano. Ash rained out across the north-western states. The top four

hundred metres of the volcano was replaced by a gaping grey amphitheatre. For the next six years, a small dome of lava pushed its way out into the new crater, until gradually the conduit was plugged and activity stopped. In all, about one cubic kilometre of rock was thrown out during the whole eruption.

Mount St Helens was a tiny eruption by global standards. Yet it taught us a lot. Until St Helens, nobody realised quite how fragile volcanic mountains are. Since then, numerous examples of volcanoes that have collapsed sideways have been recognised from the tell-tale carpet of hummocks and hills that stretch away from the remains of ancient amphitheatres. St Helens also gave an inkling

Eruption of Mt St Helens, 18th May 1980. The initial blast was horizontal, blowing the northern flank outwards.

View of what was once forest around Mt St Helens.

of the nuisance that even a small eruption can cause to a society that relies on sensitive equipment for transport, communications and day-to-day life.

CENTRAL AMERICA

Central and South America contain some of the greatest riches of the volcanic world. From Colima to Popocatepetl and the Pico de Orizaba, southern Mexico is crossed by a belt of volcanic giants that rise up to five kilometres above sea-level. Many of its small, young volcanoes remain undated. In 1982, El Chichon, a previously unknown volcano swathed in tropical vegetation, burst into life. This small eruption caused a big splash by pumping over ten million tonnes of sulphur into the atmosphere. In terms of the effect it had on the world's weather, this was the most significant eruption for nearly twenty years,

and caused a resurgence of interest in the links between explosive eruptions and changing climates.

The western regions of the Central American states are littered with volcanoes. Many of these are relatively young, with reputations still to make. Others are irrepressibly active. Santa Maria, a tall cone in Guatemala, marked the start of the twentieth century with a colossal explosive eruption. Not content with this, a dome of lava began to emerge from the flanks of the volcano just twenty years later. This dome has now been growing for seventy-five years as sticky, dacite magma pushes to the surface.

Arenal and Poas are two of Costa Rica's best known volcanoes. Arenal is a young cone that achieved notoriety in 1968, when it erupted violently after a couple of centuries of repose.

The devastation caused by the St Helens' eruption spread for miles.

It continues to offer a natural 'son et lumière' today, with small explosions scattering incandescent ash skywards several times per day. Poas is a rather older and more complex cone. The summit is a mixture of craters, with two crater lakes. The southern lake is clear. The northern lake is a vivid turquoise-green to blue colour and is highly acidic. Noxious gases trying to escape from the volcano are trapped within this northern lake. It is usually warm or hot, and its level changes continuously. It is topped up by rain, and the water level falls as water evaporates. When hot magma is near the surface, the level of the lake can fall dramatically. Occasionally, as the lake dries out, pools of molten sulphur erupt from the lake bed, throwing sprays of yellow sulphur across the crater.

SOUTH AMERICA

Three chains of volcanoes stretch along the western coast of South America. The first band runs for twelve hundred kilometres from northern Colombia to southern Ecuador. The volcanoes of this region are not well known, but are still highly dangerous.

Small eruptions at three of these volcanoes have caused some of the worst fatalities of any recent volcanic eruptions. Nevado del Ruiz is best known for its small eruption in 1985. Hot ash melted ice and snow around the summit of Ruiz. The mixture of ash, water and snow was rapidly channelled into the deep valleys that drain the volcano. Soon after, this spilled out across the surrounding plains as dense, rapidly moving mudflows that overwhelmed the town of Armero. More than two-thirds of the 29,000 residents of Armero were killed, in an event that, if not predictable, was certainly preventable.

In January 1993, nine people, including six volcanologists, were killed in an unexpected blast in the crater of Galeras volcano, in southern Colombia. There has never been a worse incident involving volcano scientists. Tragically, just two months later, two more scientists were killed in a small steam explosion at the Ecuadorian volcano, Guagua Pinchincha. Since then, there is a new awareness of the risks, and the use of safety equipment, such as fireproof suits, has become more widespread on erupting volcanoes.

The second volcanic chain stretches for another fifteen hundred kilometres from southern Peru to northern Chile. This chain includes some of the most starkly beautiful, and little studied, volcanoes of the high altiplano. These volcanoes are so remote that

Crater formed during the 1980 Mt St Helens' eruption

Eruption of the volcano Arenal, Costa Rica which occurred on 6 July 1991.

much of their history, or indeed their very existence, is known only from space shuttle photographs and satellite pictures. During the 1980's, the eruptions of one of these volcanoes, Lascar, were followed almost exclusively by satellite. Satellite images were used first to detect the heat from a glowing dome of lava deep inside one of Lascar's craters. Later pictures tracked the path across the Atacama desert of ash thrown up as an explosion blew the dome apart.

The final chain extends from central Chile to Patagonia. As elsewhere in South America,

View of the dormant Popocatapetl, the second highest volcanic peak in Mexico.

most of these volcanoes are stratocones. Their spacing is remarkably regular, with new volcanoes appearing every thirty to forty kilometres down the chain. They are also nearly all the same height. This tells us that molten rock is being formed all the way along the chain, deep in the mantle. Then, in the same way that raindrops on a window pane merge into evenly spaced trails of water that slide down the glass, the molten rock collects together before finally rising at intervals to the surface. Half-way along the chain, Villarica is a snow-clad giant, and a well-known ski resort. Eruptions in 1971-2 left trails of ropy lava across its lower flanks, stretching up to fourteen kilometres from the summit. The fountains of lava and ash rapidly melted the snow and ice around the summit, sending flash floods and mudflows roaring into the valleys around its flanks. Villarica steamed gently for the next thirteen years, before further bursts of activity in 1984 and 1985. Since then, a small lava lake has appeared intermittently in the summit crater. Fountains of fire and plumes of ash mark the appearance and disappearance of the lava lake as the magma rises and falls within the volcano.

Ash cloud formed by devastating explosive eruption at Lascar.

CHAPTER SEVEN

ASIA AND INDONESIA

From Kamchatka to the Philippines and Indonesia, the volcanoes of the Asian margin are among the most active and violent in the world. These volcanoes all owe their existence to the destruction of the Earth's tectonic plates beneath Eurasia.

The Kurile islands stretch from the Aleutians to mainland Russia. At least forty active volcanoes sprout along this island chain, and most have erupted in the last hundred years. They lie in a dangerously precarious position underneath some of the world's busiest air traffic routes. Even a small puff from any of these volcanoes can inject ash into the flight paths, eight to twelve kilometres up. As the ash trails across the Pacific Ocean with the winds, it forms a thin but deadly layer.

The Kamchatka peninsula is a volcanic paradise. Kamchatka contains many fabulous volcanoes, from the perpetually active Kliuchevskoi, through Bezymianny, a scarred, latter-day Mount St Helens, to the vast shield of Tolbachik. Further inland, across eastern and central Asia, there are a few scattered volcanoes. These lie above stretches and tears in the Eurasian plate. Baitoushan, on the Chinese - Korean border, may have been responsible for the largest eruption of the

past two thousand years. Undoubtedly, there are many more still to be discovered.

JAPAN

Few areas of Japan are far from the grasp of an active volcano. Most of Japan has been coated with volcanic ash in the last few

The deposit from a single pyroclastic flow, ninety kilometres away from the Aso volcano vent, Japan.

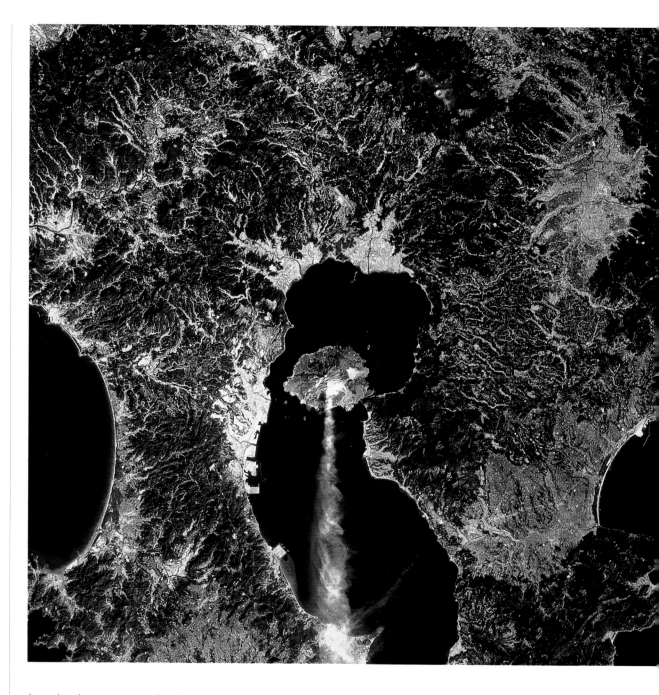

Satellite image of the Sakurajima volcano. One of the world's most active volcanoes, it has erupted thousands of times since AD 708.

hundred years, and deaths on Japanese volcanoes are still tragically frequent. The most vigorous and energetic volcanoes cluster on the southern island of Kyushu.

Aso volcano is a large caldera that has pumped out steam and ash in small explosions since at least 553 AD. Concrete shelters line the edges of the crater, to offer the many visitors some protection from falling rocks. In the past, Aso spewed vast quantities of ash and pumice across the region in four large explosions. During each, hot flows of pumice and ash tumbled from every side of the volcano, burying everything around with thick, sterile deposits. The ashy signatures of these eruptions, together with hundreds more, can be traced across Japan and out to sea.

A little further south, Sakurajima is a small cone that perches inside the flooded remains of huge crater. Sakurajima has erupted several times per week since 1955, showering nearby towns and villages with a constant rain of black volcanic sand. Sakurajima has a well-deserved place in the annals of volcanic history, since it was here that 'volcano seismology', the study of volcanic earthquakes, was born. In 1914, the earthquake scientist, Fusakichi Omori discovered that volcanoes behave like small balloons buried in the

Eruption of the Sakurajima volcano in Kagoshima Bay on the Japanese island of Kyushu in 1988.

ground. Before an eruption, the balloon fills up, putting pressure on the rocks around and above, causing them to bulge at the surface. After an eruption, the balloon and the swelling subside. Nowadays, sensitive instruments to detect this ballooning can be found on volcanoes the world over. Unfortunately, not all balloons are the same, and we have yet to learn how to tell when they will burst.

The city of Kagoshima lies across the bay from Sakurajima. Here, people clear up fallen ash and leave it for the municipal ash collectors in just the same way as people elsewhere leave their rubbish for disposal. Apart from the

inconvenience of having black ash rain down on their cars and into their swimming pools, residents of Kagoshima have little to fear from the volcano as it continues to puff. The bay that separates the city from the island is large enough to provide a buffer against almost everything that the volcano can throw out.

For the islanders who live at the foot of Sakurajima and work its fabled soil, the volcano is a bountiful provider. Here, radishes grow to the size of turnips. The frequent emergency drills, hard hats and gas masks are just as much a part of their routine as umbrellas and raincoats are in England.

Right and Opposite: Mayon, Phillippines. The 1993 lava flow forms a prominent feature running down the middle of the cone.

INDONESIA

The Indonesian archipelago hosts many of the world's most beautiful volcanoes. From the tiny peak of Bromo, that nestles inside the craters of Tengger, and against the backdrop of Semeru, to the yellow sulphur cliffs of Kawah Ijen, Java is the destination of choice for volcano tourists. Nearby islands have also seen some of the largest eruptions of the past few thousand years. Tambora, on the island of Sumbawa, erupted catastrophically in 1815. Hot pumice avalanches swept the island, killing ten thousand people. On neighbouring islands, another eighty thousand died from starvation and disease. The summer of 1816 in northern Europe, the eastern United States and China was miserably cold as a result.

The largest eruption of the past hundred thousand years formed Lake Toba in Sumatra. Seventy-four thousand years ago, Toba threw over six thousand cubic kilometres of ash across the Indian ocean. Even today, ash ten centimetres thick can still be found in mainland India. This eruption was many times larger than the largest eruption of the past two hundred years, and the effects were enormous. Toba threw up so much volcanic pollution that the chemical composition of the atmosphere was changed. Droplets of volcanic sulphur remained suspended in the atmosphere for six or seven years, cooling the Earth dramatically, although this eruption does not seem to have had a lasting effect on the planet. As Toba erupted, the globe was already moving into an ice-age. Indeed, this might well have been the factor that caused the volcano

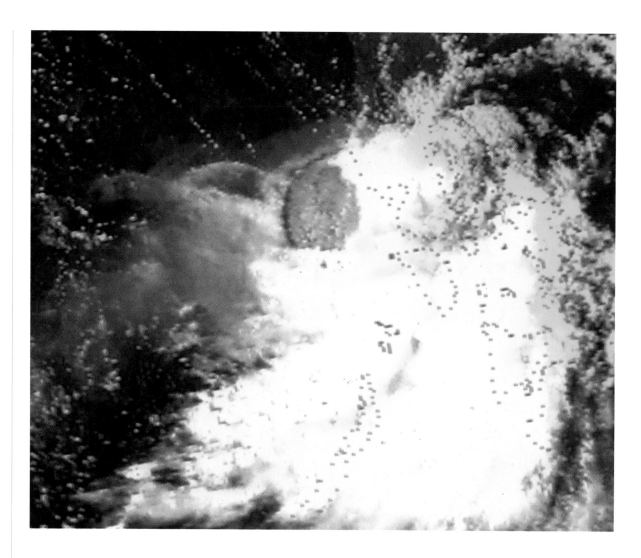

Satellite image of the plinian ash plume from the eruption of Mt Pinatubo bursting through thick cloud, 14 June 1991.

to erupt. The rate of cooling may have been speeded up by the eruption, but in the end the ice-age was no colder, or longer, than any other.

KRAKATAU, INDONESIA

Krakatau gave the world some inkling of the power of volcanoes when it erupted in 1883. Before the eruption, Krakatau was a typical volcanic island, made up of several overlapping cones and craters. Unrest began at one of the three main cones in May 1883, spreading to the next a month later. By early August, all three cones were puffing ash. The island lay on the main sailing route from Europe to the East, at the entrance to the

Sunda Straits, so there were frequent reports as the eruption developed. On August 26th, the main phase of eruption began, and built to a climax on August 27th. In Jakarta, ash began to fall early in the morning. By 11 a.m. it was completely dark. The smell of sulphur and gritty ash was everywhere. At midday, a five-metre high wave swept into the port. This was the first burst of the tsunami that accompanied the eruption. A larger wave swept through two hours later.

The first reports telegraphed to London told a sorry tale. "All gone. Plenty lives lost," was the message from Serang. Other reports said that thirty-metre 'tidal' waves (or tsunami) had swept the western coasts of Java and Sumatra.

The eight hundred metre tall island of Krakatau had disappeared, and sixteen new islands had appeared at the entrance of the Sunda Straits. Later the same day, the tsunami arrived in San Francisco, and a two metre wave swept into Perth harbour. The noise of the eruption is legendary. At the northern tip of Sumatra, seventeen hundred kilometres away, troops rushed outside thinking their fort was under attack. Pressure waves from the eruption circled the globe seven times, like waves in a tea-cup.

The ash cloud caused widespread hazes as it sped round the globe in late August. This haze dulled the sun, making it appear no brighter than the moon, and surrounding it with a rusty-red corona. Thousands of kilometres away from Krakatau, ash continued to fall for several days.

By early November the official death toll approached 33,000. Many had drowned in the enormous tsunami. Others were killed by the hot flows of ash and pumice that sped across the sea from the volcano. Some of these flows crossed eighty kilometres of open ocean in less than an hour, and were still hot enough to burn people and huts on the Sumatran coast.

The stories of the disappearance of the island turned out to be only partly correct. In fact, the eruption threw out twelve cubic kilometres of molten rock, forming a new six kilometre-wide submerged crater. The old island was cut in two. The 'new islands' turned out to be beds, two or three metres thick, of

Pyroclastic sand sea, twenty-five kilometres from Mt Pinatubo.

hot floating pumice that clogged the Sunda Straits. Enormous rafts of pumice drifted hundreds of kilometres across the Indian Ocean over the next few months, before sinking to the ocean floor. About the same time, fantastic sunsets illuminated the northern hemisphere. By March 1884, vegetation was springing back to life in places where the old soil hadn't been too deeply buried, and villagers in the worst-affected parts of Java and Sumatra began to rebuild their lives. The largest eruption for two generations was over, and Krakatau slept for the next forty years.

THE PHILIPPINES

The tropical islands of the Philippines are dotted with active volcanoes. The climate means that even the youngest volcanoes are heavily forested, and little is known of their history before the arrival of Magellan in 1521. More eruptions in the Philippines have been responsible for death and destruction than anywhere else in the world. In recent years, however, many more lives have been saved by well-planned evacuations.

Like many tropical islands, the effects of eruptions in the Philippines are often worsened by heavy rain. Mudflows are a long-standing problem, as tropical storms can loosen large quantities of ash and pumice from the steep slopes, and send ash-laden floods across the surrounding plains. Volcanic mudflows are often called 'lahars'; the Indonesian term for lava. Mudflow is an inadequate description, as many of these flows are nothing like mud. Instead, they flow with the consistency of cement, at the temperature of boiling water and can carry boulders the size of small cars.

The volcanoes of Mayon, Pinatubo and Taal provide spectacular illustrations of the devastating power of a volcanic eruption.

MAYON

Mayon is the archetypal volcanic beauty. It lies in the fertile south of Luzon, the largest island of the Philippines. It is a classical cone that rises gently up through plantations of coconuts and bananas, steepening sharply at the summit. Mayon overlooks the gulf of Albay, and over a million people live in the cities around its base. Like many volcanoes of this kind, Mayon's beauty belies its natural destructiveness. Over the past century it has

Mayon provides spectacular illustration of the power of a volcanic eruption

erupted eleven times, often with fatal results. Before the last eruption, the cone was almost perfectly symmetrical. Then, in February 1993, it burst into life again without warning. A small, violent ash and rock flow descended the Bonga valley, the deepest valley on the volcano's sides. It travelled quickly and without a sound. When the ash cloud reached the fields that lined the Bonga valley it was lunch-time, and the farmers were resting. Seventy five people were overwhelmed and killed instantly. Many were struck by large flying blocks, others suffocated in the ash-clogged cloud. It is not usual for eruptions to start completely without warning. Often, there are earth tremors, as the hot rock moves towards the surface, pushing other rocks out of the way. Or else more and more steam billows from the vent, as hot magma heats up and boils off the water that fills the fractures of the volcano. This fatal explosion of Mayon was probably caused by the quiet build up of steam below the surface. The eruption continued for another two months, as a thick lava flow spilt into the top of the Bonga valley, marring the symmetry of the cone. Mayon rumbles on today, a dull-red glow in the crater occasionally visible at night.

PINATUBO, PHILIPPINES

The eruption of Mount Pinatubo in 1991 was one of the success stories of modern volcanology. Pinatubo erupted after a long period of quiet, and covered some of the most fertile agricultural land in the Philippines with huge amounts of volcanic ash and pumice. The Pinatubo eruption was one of the largest of the past century, yet casualties were remarkably few. Less than a thousand died, while a quarter of a million people were evacuated to safety.

Before 1991, Pinatubo was just one of a number of undistinguished peaks in the Zambales mountains. These form a line of deeply dissected crags that overlook the central plains of Luzon. Pinatubo wasn't really known as a volcano, but was used as a source of geothermal energy and as a wilderness area for military training. It was something of a surprise therefore, when earthquakes began to shudder beneath the mountain in March 1991. Within three weeks, on April 2nd 1991, the first steam explosion occurred, stretching along a fracture that extended away from the summit of the mountain. Perhaps because they had two military bases nearby, at Clark air base and Subic Bay, the United States' response was rapid. Geologists from the United States' volcanic response team joined up with Filipino scientists to install monitoring equipment across the volcano. Soon it was clear that Pinatubo was a volcano with a dangerous profile. Only five hundred years earlier, dense flows had raced off the volcano. These filled valleys fifteen kilometres long with thick, hot deposits of pumice.

By early June, scientists had produced a hazard map, and evacuation plans were in hand. Tremors increased in size, and appeared to come from a small area below the summit. This was the first indication that Pinatubo was approaching meltdown. On June 7th, molten lava started to push out slowly from the summit. Ash clouds and tremors became more and more intense. The explosive phase of the eruption began soon after. Between June 12th and 15th, seventeen explosions sent ash and pumice higher and higher into the air. Then they merged into the eruption climax. For the next nine hours, ash clouds were pumped to between twenty-five and thirty kilometres in the air. Much of this collapsed as avalanches of hot pumice around the volcano.

A huge smoke and ash
plume rises from Mayon

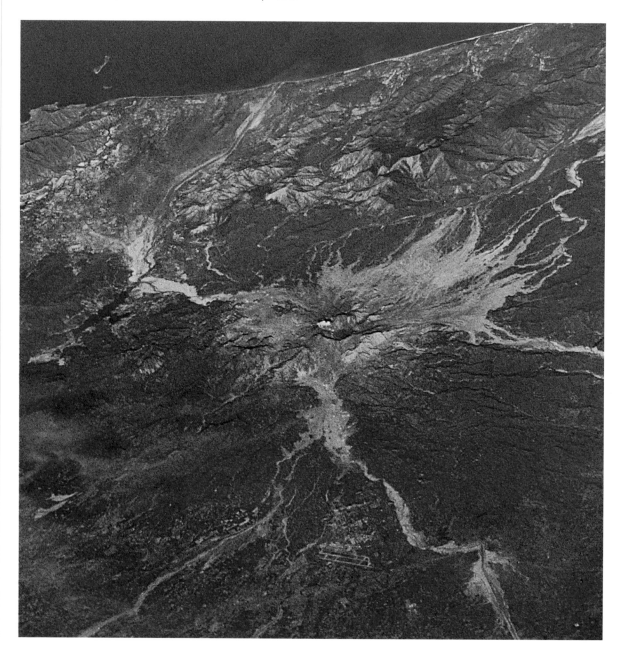

Ten cubic kilometres of pumice and ash were thrown out, and a crater two and a half kilometres wide opened up at the summit. In a twist of coincidence, the drama of the eruption coincided with the arrival of Typhoon Yunga. Torrents of rain combined with the thick, soft ash and pumice to form huge, boiling mudflows.

Much of the volcanic ash was injected high into the atmosphere. This ash cloud spread rapidly, reaching Singapore a day later, and circulating the globe in twenty-two days. Within a day of the ash cloud forming, a dozen aircraft lost power as they flew straight into it. In the worst cases, turbines seized as ash was sucked in, melting and coating the insides of the engine. Several aicraft plummeted for thousands of feet before the engines spluttered back to life and they could limp to safety.

Mount Pinatubo and its surroundings seen from space. The crater is seen right of centre.

Closer to the volcano, the eruption had a huge impact. More than two million people lived within the potential danger area, with a third of a million living within forty kilometres of the summit. Many of those who lived close were evacuated, but some of the Aeta people who lived on the volcano were reluctant to leave. Some believed that their god, Apo Namalyari, would protect them. Others were worried to leave livestock and crops as harvest time approached.

In the first year, eighty thousand houses in three hundred and fifty villages were damaged or destroyed. Although the main eruption was over by early July 1991, this was just the start of the problems for the communities around the volcano. The explosions left rock, ash and pumice hundreds of metres deep, covering tens of square kilometres of the high mountain. Deep tropical valleys were transformed into flat white seas of pumice. Rain, coming in bursts, sent muddy flow after muddy flow of water and pumice cascading down new valleys. Soon, more than four hundred square kilometres of the surrounding lowlands had been buried under thick drifts of pumice and ash. Whole villages were submerged under metres of mud and ash. Controversial attempts to control the flooding by building dykes were only partially, and temporarily, successful.

Some years after the end of the eruption, its legacy lives on. The thick pumice plains that filled the upper valleys of the mountain are now deeply scored. Huge cliffs of loose pumice perch high above the streams that drain the volcano. Storms undercut these cliffs, sending torrents of ash-laden water gushing downstream. Sometimes these events are accompanied by violent explosions, as many deposits are still considerably hotter than the boiling point of water. Lahars still move vast quantities of ash and pumice towards the sea. On the plains around the volcano, once vigorous rivers have been reduced to trickles that twist across sandy seas of white pumice. Many of the old rivers have been diverted by the thick new deposits. In Angeles City, and elsewhere, houses look curiously stunted, their lower levels buried under metres of rock.

TAAL

Manila, the capital city of the Philippines, sprawls across a plain of volcanic debris. Some of this debris is young 'ignimbrite' - thick deposits of ash and pumice, erupted as a violent, dense pumice and ash flow. Some of these flows probably erupted within the past few thousand years from nearby Lake Taal. Although it is only fifty kilometres out of central Manila, it takes a hair-raising couple of hours to reach the clean air and fabulous views of the crater rim at Taal. Pyroclastic flows would have no difficulty in making the return journey in half an hour.

Today, the greatest threat from Taal is not a of large eruption, but of a repeat of one of the many small eruptions such as it suffered during the 1960's and 1970's. The first of these, in 1965, led to the discovery of a new type of volcanic eruption. The active volcano lies on a small island in the middle of the lake, and is a flooded crater. On September 28, 1965, a fountain of lava started to build a small cinder cone on the island. Ash plumes rose high into the sky. As water entered the vent, the eruption became highly explosive, and hot, wet clouds of ash raced away from the island and across lake Taal. Observers noticed the close similarity between the shapes of these ash clouds and the clouds formed by

Evidence of volcanic activity surrounds Taal

The dormant Taal

nuclear explosions at sea. These hot, wet flows, known as 'surges' moved with extraordinary violence. Trees were ripped from the ground and sand-blasted clean. Boats full of fleeing victims were engulfed and destroyed. Surges are much less concentrated than other sorts of pyroclastic flow. They are also less easily contained by valleys and cliffs. Fortunately, they tend to run out of energy quickly, so they don't usually travel more than a few kilometres. Surges from Taal piled up sand-dunes of volcanic debris metres deep around the shores. Since this eruption, similar dunes have been found at many volcanoes around the world. Now, more than twenty years since the last explosion at Lake Taal, the lake and the volcano are great tourist attractions. Although

the volcano is now closely monitored, there may not be much warning before a future eruption. Even a tiny explosion would once again threaten the farming and fishing communities around the shores of Lake Taal.

CHAPTER EIGHT

AFRICA AND THE MIDDLE EAST

Geologically, Africa is one of the oldest parts of the world. Many regions here can trace their roots back for two or three billion years. Africa also sits on one of the slowest-moving of the tectonic plates. All of the active volcanoes in Africa lie either along the great East African Rift valley, or else over a hotspot in the mantle below. The Middle East has few active volcanoes, and none that have had an eruption of note in the recent past.

Southern Africa hasn't seen an eruption for nearly ninety million years, but what eruptions they must have been! Some of the most interesting volcanoes of the region are made of 'kimberlite'. This is a strange material that was once rich in carbon dioxide that formed deep within the Earth. During eruptions, small

Kerimasi Volcano, East African Rift.

Apollo 9 photograph of the Afar Triangle in Djibouti, East Africa. This area is where three of the great rift systems of the Earth's crust meet.

amounts of molten kimberlite burst its way through the crust, forming a slender carrot-shaped vent one or two kilometres deep. Because kimberlite rises quickly from great depths, it usually brings with it fragments of exotic rocks and minerals. The most coveted of these are diamonds. Diamonds form deep below the most ancient parts of the continents. Here the pressures are high, but the temperatures are still low enough for carbon to bond strongly into this most desirable form. Flawed diamonds are often of most interest to geologists. The flaws can be droplets of frozen melt, or fragments of

minerals, which are the deepest samples that we have from Earth's interior. Kimberlite magmas that contain diamonds can be found in many places around the world where the crust is ancient and undisturbed.

Traces of ancient volcanic eruptions can also be found across half a million square kilometres of south-eastern Africa. This is the enormous Karroo basin, which was first flooded with basalt lavas between about two hundred and one hundred and fifty million years ago. Although many of the lavas have been eroded away, the pipes and fissures that fed these lavas still exist. Reconstructions of the Karroo show that this was an enormous region, once covered by lava several kilometres thick. These lavas are quite similar to those found in the Columbia River of the north-western United States, or the Deccan region of India. The Karroo basalts formed as the continent of Antarctica was torn away from Africa and India in the death throes of the giant continent of Gondwana.

Huge volcanic massifs form the mountains of Hoggar and Tibesti in southern Algeria and northern Chad. Volcanoes in the Tibesti are large, young calderas. From space, these stand out as a blot of black in the middle of the yellow expanse of the Sahara desert. Like Yellowstone, in the United States, these volcanoes lie over a hot spot that rises deep within the Earth. Unlike Yellowstone however, Tibesti is rarely visited and little known.

THE EAST AFRICAN RIFT VALLEY

The East African Rift valley is a huge feature that cuts deep through eastern Africa, from Eritrea to Malawi. The rift is a tear in the Earth's crust, where the African plate is slowly being pulled apart. In the far north, the desert region of the Afar marks the point where three plates join together. This is the location of some of the world's most fascinating and remote volcanoes, in the fabled Danakil desert. Some of these volcanoes barely rise above sea level. Others, like Erta 'Ale, form large, low shields with glowing ponds of lava filling small craters in the summit.

As the rift valley stretches inland through Ethiopia, its is lined by huge and relatively unknown cones, shields and craters. At least

Ariel view of the Oldoinyo Lengai crater, Tanzania.

fifty of these volcanoes are thought to be still active, although none have any recorded eruptions. The earliest humans grew up near the lava fields and volcanoes of Ethiopia, and their remains are now preserved beneath some of the many ash layers that fill the rift valley. The cones and shields continue through Kenya, from the practically-named Barrier that blocks the southern end of lake Turkana, to the lyrical Emuruangogolak. The rift valley begins to die away in Tanzania. Huge volcanoes like Kilimanjaro and Meru tower over the eastern edge of the rift. To the West, giant abandoned craters like Ngorongoro flank the Serengeti plateau, providing natural reserves for rich and diverse wild life.

OLDOINYO LENGAI, TANZANIA

Oldoinyo Lengai rises majestically from the western edge of the Tanzanian rift valley. The volcano looks like a scarred cone, with a pair of craters on either side of its triangular summit peak. In 1914, a German volcanologist, Hans Reck, climbed to the summit and returned with reports of bizarre volcanic pinnacles and bubbling mud pools. It wasn't until fifty years later that the unique character of the volcano was fully recognised. In 1960 a British geologist, Barry Dawson, abseiled into the crater to collected some samples for analysis. At that time the crater looked like a partly retracted piston. It was several hundred

Fresh lava flows at Oldoinyo Lengai, 1993.

Oldoinyo Lengai

metres across, with vertical cliffs dropping a hundred metres to the crater floor. The floor of the crater sported a couple of volcanic pimples, with black, brown and white flows spilling gently out of each vent. Unlike all other lavas which are mostly made of silica, these lavas turned out to contain no silica. Instead they have the same composition as washing soda, and contain sodium and potassium carbonate.

In spite of its very curious composition, Oldoinyo Lengai seems to behave like most other volcanoes. The latest activity began with a small explosion in 1983. It was five years before the first scientific expeditions climbed to the summit. By late 1988, the northern crater of the volcano was less than thirty metres deep, and covered in fresh lava. Half a dozen steaming and gushing vents emerged

from the crater floor. The noise was terrific. There were explosions every two or three seconds as large bubbles burst from a small brown lava pond, scattering droplets of frozen melt over a small cinder cone. Lava slopped and gurgled in the pond, day and night. tinting everything in the surrounding area sombre shades of brown. These lavas are molten, but they only have a temperature of about six hundred degrees Celsius. This is about five hundred degrees cooler than Hawaiian lava. Only at night do the Lengai lavas glow a very dull orange.

The whole eruption was like a scaled down version of Hawaii. Molten carbonate is much closer to water than basalt in its behaviour. The tiniest pahoehoe lava flows are just centimetres thick, creeping and spilling over the ground. The thickest aa flows are still just

tens of centimetres thick, edging forward across the crater floor. In a burst of activity in 1993, a bubbling cone of lava formed and collapsed. Five-metre thick flows, rich in minerals that are only known to exist at this one place on Earth, spilled across half of the crater floor. Lava has continued to pour out of the volcano since then, and the crater is now precariously full. It cannot be too long before the first flows spill over the edge. Curiously, Oldoinyo Lengai is intimately linked with the life cycle of the flamingo. The caustic lakes of Natron and Magadi lie just a few kilometres away from Lengai, on the rift floor. Flamingos feed on the sparse lake fauna, and build their nests in the soda crusts of these two lakes. Volcanic ash that has been scattered from Lengai in the past is the source of much of this sodium carbonate.

NYIRAGONGO

Two volcanic peaks stretch up from the edge of the Virunga mountains on the western side of the African Rift. Both of these volcanoes, Nyamuragira and Nyiragongo, are prolific lava producers. Nyiragongo has a lake of lava perched within the crater, where layers of frozen lava inside the crater mark past levels of the lake, like thick tidemarks. The lava lake was first seen when the volcano was discovered in 1894, and it remained a permanent feature until January 1977, when the lake drained without warning through a fracture in the side of the volcano. In less than an hour, tens of millions of cubic metres of lava rushed down the sides of the volcano. The level of the lava lake dropped by over five hundred metres. Because the lavas were very fluid, they were able to flow exceptionally fast, at about sixty kilometres per hour. Seventy

people and numerous animals were engulfed. The lava lake reappeared in mid-1982, and has remained there ever since.

VOLCANOES OF THE CAMEROON

A small line of volcanoes run through the West African country of Cameroon. Only two of these, Mt. Cameroon and Santa Isabel, have erupted this century. Better known, though, are the tragic events in the Oku volcanic field in north Cameroon. This is a region of small crater volcanoes. These craters, known as 'maars', form where small amounts of lava erupt through wet rock in violent eruptions of steam and ash. Lake Nyos fills one of these maars. In August 1986, a cloud of carbon dioxide poured out of lake Nyos. This dense,

choking cloud swept through villages below Nyos, suffocating seventeen hundred people as a result. There was no warning, nor any eruption.

The lake, like many volcanic lakes, is fed continuously by warm, gas-charged springs from below. As long as the lake is stable, more and more gas can dissolve in the bottom of the lake. Once the lake starts to overturn, the gas bubbles quickly out of the lake, sending a surge of gas and water bursting over the shallow lip of the crater. This sort of behaviour is probably just part of the life-cycle of this and other tropical volcanic lakes. At Nyos efforts have now been made to let the gas escape gradually, rather than build up, in an attempt to break this deadly cycle.

Active vents on the crater floor. Oldoinyo Lengai, 1998.

A lake has filled the crater at Kimberley

CHAPTER NINE

AUSTRALASIA

The islands of Melanesia and New Zealand complete the long chain of volcanoes of the Pacific Ring of Fire. Like their counterparts in Asia and America, many of these volcanoes have dramatic pasts, and remain active today.

Set back from the edges of the plate, Australia has not seen an eruption since before Captain James Cook's arrival in the late eighteenth century. Despite this, it does have some young volcanoes, and a long history of ancient eruptions, stretching back billions of years.

Western Australia is a huge expanse of ancient rock. The gently rolling hills are part of a landscape that has taken three hundred million years to form. The rocks here formed as volcanoes almost three billion years ago, when the continents were still young and the face of the Earth was quite different from today. This region is rich in nickel, copper and platinum. Ancient granites are criss-crossed by lodes laden with gold. Three billion years ago the Earth was much hotter than today. The lavas that erupted then are called komatiites. Komatiites are black, like basalt, and are mostly made of silicon, oxygen and magnesium. They were hotter, and far more fluid than any lavas today. Komatiites would have made deep, fast-flowing and turbulent rivers of lava, glowing intensely red-hot. In fact, komatiite was so hot when it erupted that it could melt the rocks around the volcano. So, like pouring melted chocolate over ice-cream, komatiite lava melted itself into deep channels. Further away from the volcano the channels became shallower as the lava cooled.

Komatiites cooled very quickly. Like basalts, komatiites grew crystals of a mineral called olivine as they cooled. Usually olivine grows into squat crystals. In komatiites, however, olivine formed into long, wispy and hollow crystals, because it grew too fast to make the usual crystal shape. Komatiites haven't erupted in any quantity for two billion years, so we have to be content with basalts, which are tame by comparison.

TAUPO, NEW ZEALAND

Lake Taupo, in the centre of New Zealand's North Island, hides a mammoth volcano. Nearly two thousand years ago, around 180 AD, Taupo erupted with tremendous violence. At first, ash and pumice fought its way through a small lake. A plume rose thirty kilometres into the air, and rained wet mud and ash all around. As the eruption continued, the lake dried out and the ash and pumice rose fifty kilometres above the volcano. This is the highest an eruption cloud is able to rise on Earth. This was just the beginning. As the plume of ash collapsed, it turned into a dense cloud that rushed away from all sides of the vent. These flows left a deposit just a few metres thick, and travelled eighty kilometres away from the volcano, in all directions, in just a few minutes.

The eruption at Taupo was just the last of many over the past two hundred thousand years. Taupo's history shows that it is unpredictable, and we have no clues as to when, or how big, the next eruption might be. Fortunately for us, giant eruptions at caldera volcanoes like Taupo are very rare, and usually spaced thousands of years apart.

RUAPEHU

Ruapehu is a ragged conical volcano, and the tallest peak on New Zealand's North Island. It is also a major ski resort. Together with its conical neighbour, Ngauruhoe, which last erupted in the late 1970's, Ruapehu lies in the

Ruapehu

Eruption of Ngauruhoe 1975

away from Ruapehu. Three months later, on a clear September day, more explosions rocked the resort. Each blast sent rocks, water and ash hundreds of metres into the sky, and set off meltwater lahars around the mountain. Further explosions sent plumes of ash high into the air, and scattered a film of ash across much of the North island. Although the ash contained some nutrients, it also contained lethal fluorine compounds that killed several thousand grazing sheep.

By the middle of October the crater lake had dried out. Explosions continued infrequently for the next nine months, before the activity finally died down and the crater lake refilled. Little of this eruption will be preserved in the geological record, and its effects will only be short-lived.

RABAUL

The town of Rabaul, in New Britain, has one of the finest natural harbours of the South Pacific, overlooked by the twin volcanic peaks of Vulcan and Tavurvur. The presence of the harbour is no coincidence, as it is the rim of the old volcanic crater, or caldera, which was formed by a number of colossal eruptions during the past twenty thousand years. The last really large eruption from Rabaul, about 1400 years ago, may have been responsible for widespread environmental damage at around 536 AD. Across the northern hemisphere crops failed and there was widespread drought and famine, similar to the effects that followed the Tambora eruption of 1815.

Rabaul has had many small eruptions since 1767. The most significant of these, in May 1937, lasted for three days and left five hundred dead and the town in tatters. In the

Tongariro national park. Since 1946, the crater at the summit of Ruapehu has been filled with hot water. Even during winter, heat from the volcano keeps the lake warm. In the 1950's the lake was a big draw for bathing tourists, until it evolved into a diluted sulphuric acid bath. So much sulphur is pumped into the lake by the volcano that pools of molten sulphur line the bottom of the lake.

Ruapehu erupts frequently, and its eruptions are usually small. The bursts of activity in 1995 and 1996 were typical of events that occur at this volcano every few decades. The first sign that anything was out of the ordinary came on June 29th, 1995. A small explosion under the lake threw hot water, mud and rocks onto the snow-capped top of the volcano. Some snow and ice melted, and cool mudflows slid into the rivers, draining the volcano. Slurries of snow were found as far as forty kilometres early 1980's earthquake activity resumed. Many of the tremors came from fractures near the edge of the caldera. There was some concern that this might be the start of a large eruption, but the tremors peaked in 1984 and then stopped. With hindsight this was a life-saver, as the experience proved to be a dry run for what happened next. At 3 a.m. on Sunday September 18th, 1994, a magnitude 5.1 earthquake shook the town. A small tsunami washed through the bay. After an earthquake of that size it is usual to feel some aftershocks, but in this case the tremors became more and more frequent. The thirty

Ngauruhoe

Smoke plume from the 1994 eruption on Rabaul, New Guinea, seen during a Space Shuttle Mission.

thousand residents of Rabaul took this as their cue to evacuate. By 2 a.m. on September 19th, one or two quakes were being felt every minute, and most of Rabaul was deserted. As the sun rose, it was clear that an eruption was about to start, and parts of the harbour had been lifted six metres out of the sea. Soon after 6 a.m., only twenty-seven hours after the first warning, ash and steam began to pour from Tavurvur. An hour later Vulcan, a cone that only appeared in 1878, joined the fray. For the first couple of hours the vents warmed up. Wet clouds of ash collapsed from the sides of small rising plumes, showering areas up to two kilometres away with damp powdered rock. By 8.30 a.m., Rabaul was blacked out under a pall of ash. For the next two hours ash clouds accelerated, reaching eighteen kilometres high in the air. Torrential rain fell with the ash, coating buildings thickly with mud. Tens of centimetres of wet ash fell across Rabaul, and roofs started to collapse. The peak of the eruption was over by 11 a.m.

Outside Rabaul, which was by now cut off from the outside world, stories raced electronically around the globe. There were tales of five vents having opened up, of an island disappearing, and of complete devastation. The reality was a little less dramatic. The eruption continued for some days, the two vents playing harmonising tunes. Pumice from Vulcan clogged the bay with a thick, floating raft of debris. Ash billowed from both vents, rising just a couple of kilometres above the sea. Eventually Vulcan sputtered to a halt in early October. Tavurvur slowly squeezed out a couple of lava flows, and went into a decline that finished in late December. The whole caldera gently subsided, and ended up between 20 centimetres and a metre deeper than it had been three months before.

The prompt evacuation of Rabaul kept casualties to a minimum, although troops were called in soon after to keep looters at bay. Four people died as their houses collapsed over them, a man was killed by lightning, and a boy was killed by a truck during the evacuation. The two volcanoes have rumbled on and off since 1995, but the threat of a large eruption seems to have passed.

Viewing the smoking vent of Ngauruhoe

EREBUS

The vast continent of Antarctica boasts only a handful of volcanoes. Four are known to have erupted since 1900. Of these, Erebus is the largest and most active. It is also the southernmost active volcano in the world. Erebus towers three thousand metres above the Ross ice shelf. The summit crater is brimming with hot, fluid lava. Enormous white crystals of feldspar float in the lava, like chips in a deep-fat fryer. As gas bubbles rise through the lava lake and burst, showers of volcanic glass, lumps of lava and crystals are scattered out of the crater and over the top of the cone. Bubbles burst several times a day, usually releasing enough energy to be spotted on the sensitive earthquake recorders that surround the volcano. More violent bursts occasionally throw metre-sized, twisted shards of material, like giant scraps of dough, around the summit.

Like the volcanoes with lava lakes elsewhere, Erebus has probably been in this state for many years, pumping noxious fumes into the clean Antarctic air.

Katabaric Wind scouring the slopes of Erebus

CHAPTER TEN

CARIBBEAN

The green tropical islands of the Lesser Antilles stretch northwards from Grenada. This is the Caribbean volcanic arc. Deep below, rocks of the Atlantic sea-floor dip steeply underneath the Caribbean Plate. The rocks being destroyed here are some of the oldest on the ocean floor. They date back to the time when Africa and the Americas were first separated, and the Atlantic ocean formed.

The sixteen known volcanoes of the Lesser Antilles have an unenviable record of eruptions. Nine of the volcanoes have erupted since the late seventeenth century, including five since 1900, and over thirty thousand people have died as a result.

Caribbean eruptions are particularly well-known for two aspects: 'nuées ardentes' and domes. The eruptions in 1902 of the Soufrière

left and over page: Views of the lava dome, Montserrat, March 1998. This dome is over 200 metres tall, and the summit height is over 1000 metres.

*See previous page
for caption*

of St Vincent and Mont Pelée on Martinique were among the first recognised examples of 'nuée ardentes'. Nuées, or literally 'burning clouds' are better known as pyroclastic flows, or 'block and ash flows'. They are simply the familiar hot rock and ash avalanches that race down the sides of a volcano during explosive eruptions. A single nuée ardente razed the city of St Pierre, Martinique, to the ground in just a few minutes on the morning of May 8, 1902. The two survivors were a shoemaker, who escaped death on the fringes of the city, and Louis-Auguste Ciparis. Ciparis had spent the night of May 7th incarcerated in prison. The cell was very securely built, partly below ground, and without windows. Any less sturdy, and this building too would have been destroyed. Ciparis was found, burned and parched with thirst, four days later. Following the explosions of May 8th, Mont Pelée

continued to erupt sticky lava as a large, spiny dome for the next three years. A more recent dome-forming eruption started on Montserrat in 1995, and old domes are found on many of the Lesser Antilles.

MONTSERRAT, WEST INDIES

Montserrat is one of the smallest islands of the Lesser Antilles. Ancient eruptions, over the past three million years, had given the island its distinctive hilly appearance, but before the latest eruption began, in July 1995, there had been no historical activity. Most of Montserrat is made of steep, overlapping domes of highly sticky lava. Individual domes can be up to five hundred metres tall, and one or two kilometres across. Each of the mountains on the island is made from several domes and their scree slopes.

In the 1930's and the late 1960's, lots of small earthquakes were felt across the island. These earthquakes originated under the Soufrière Hills, so called because of the hot sulphurous springs around the mountain. Similar hot-springs, also known as soufrières, are found across the Lesser Antilles. From 1992 to 1995 there was another burst of earthquake activity. This time the quakes were followed, on July 18th 1995, by bursts of steam and ash from English's crater in the Soufrière Hills. One month later, the first large explosion blanketed the capital, Plymouth, in ash, prompting the first evacuation of people from southern Montserrat.

Since then, the eruption has continued without stopping, and has gradually increased in violence and size. The eruption of Montserrat has taught us a vast amount about rare, dome-forming eruptions. The eruption has also been quite different from the short but very dramatic eruptions of Mount St Helens and Mount Pinatubo.

The eruption began to settle down into a steady pattern in late 1995. By late September the first spine of lava appeared in the crater. By late November, hot, glowing lava had started to fill English's crater. Montserrat lava is called andesite. This is richer in silicon than basalt, and is exceedingly sticky. As it squeezes out of the vent it is not able to flow very well, and instead piles up into a huge mass of boulders. For much of the time the eruption can barely be detected. Since early 1996, between two and eight cubic metres of lava has squeezed to the surface every second. This is somewhere between a small car-load and a truck-load of rock. The amount of new lava perched on top of the volcano is now so large that noticeable changes in the shape and

Ash clouds spreading across the island of Montserrat, February 1998.

Plymouth, once the capital of Montserrat, abandoned since early 1996 and hit by pyroclastic flows in 1997.

lava pours out of the vent to form a dome. After two or three months the dome has become so large that the lava has difficulty erupting. The large size of the dome also means that it pushes harder and harder on the sides of the old volcano. The dome, and other parts of the volcano, start to show the strain by crumbling, sending first falls of rock, and then larger and larger avalanches of hot rock down the sides of the volcano. On June 25th, 1997, after a couple of weeks of increasing activity, three huge avalanches raced off the mountain in the early afternoon. The avalanches, or flows, moved off the volcano at two hundred kilometres per hour. The flows, and ash clouds with them, rushed over farmland in the centre of the island, devastating three villages on the way, before finally stopping on the edges of the airport. Nineteen people died in the flows. Ten of the bodies have never been recovered. Several dozen escaped with their lives from the edges of the destroyed area. One ran barefoot into the next valley. Another drove, with all four car tyres alight, until he reached safety. Others were plucked, burnt but alive, from the ruins of their homes. Within hours, a new dome started to form in the scar left by this event. On September 21, 1997, and again on December 26, 1997, there were more large collapse events, more landslides and more violent flows. In both cases, a new dome started growing soon after.

During the first few months of 1998 the dome-growing activity continued. If the new dome eventually grows as large as the ancient domes on the island, the eruption will probably continue for another couple of years.

While this sort of long-lasting behaviour is relatively unusual, there are a few more

size of the volcano can usually only be seen with the naked eye from week to week.

Since mid-1997 the eruption has become more dangerous, simply because the dome has become so large. English's crater no longer exists. Now it is completely full of lava, and the new lava mass towers above all of the older peaks on the island. In September 1996, there was a huge landslide of rock from the growing dome, followed by a short burst of explosive activity. This triggered large pyroclastic flows, and cast ash across wide areas of the island. Similar events have happened every three months since April 1997, building up to a recognisable pattern. First,

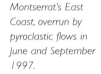

Montserrat's East Coast, overrun by pyroclastic flows in June and September 1997.

extreme volcanoes around the world. At Santa Maria, in Guatemala, a dome of lava began to form in 1922, just twenty years after a large explosive eruption of the same volcano. This lava dome, now called Santiaguito, is still growing.

SOUFRIÈRE OF ST VINCENT

Like many of the other Caribbean volcanoes, St Vincent has long boasted a steaming, sulphurous Soufrière. The soufrière has erupted violently four times since the start of the eighteenth century. The first of these was in March 1718. Daniel Defoe, the author of 'Robinson Crusoe', pieced together a colourful account of the eruption from correspondents in Barbados and Martinique. In the 'Saturday Post', a weekly magazine, he made a dramatic announcement. '...the entire desolation of the island of St Vincent in a manner the likes of which never happened since

Measuring the size of the dome, Montserrat, March 1998.

the Deluge. Flames of fire like lightning came out of the Earth. The air darkened in a dreadful manner over all the islands within 100 miles. There were innumerable chimes of thunder, only the noise was a thousand times as loud. In the afternoon [came] the falling of something as thick as smoke, as fine as dust and yet solid as *sand. At Barbados it is frightful. The island of Martinique is covered.'*

Other rumours, that the island had completely disappeared, proved to be unfounded.

There was a repeat of these events when, on May 1st 1812, darkness was reported from Barbados to Nevis. Again, there are vivid eye-witness accounts.

'The mountain burst forth in a tremendous blaze, throwing up huge spouts of fire and burning stones, and throwing down its sides torrents of burning matter and scattering in the air large pieces of rock. The brilliancy of the flames had a most sublime and awful effect, and the burning stones resembled the stars in a rocket.'

Another described the effects on the people living at the foot of the mountain.

' They abandoned everything and fled towards town. Birds fell to the ground, overpowered with showers of ashes, and not a blade of grass was to be found. At three o'clock a rolling on the roofs of the houses indicated a fall of stones. The break of day dawned like a day of judgement. A chaotic gloom enveloped the mountain, and an impenetrable haze hung over the sea'.

Again, despite the damage, recovery was relatively rapid. The eruptions of 1902 to 1903 were also extremely damaging. However, they have often been overlooked as a result of the even more devastating eruption of Mont Pelée on the neighbouring island of Martinique just one day later. On

Soufriere Volcano

May 7, 1902, the first and most destructive of the sequence of eruptions began. Soon after 10 a.m., clouds of ash and steam billowed from the volcanic crater lake. By 3 p.m., what sounded like artillery fire was heard in Barbados. Soon after, fine volcanic ash started falling in Barbados. On St Vincent itself, ash had started to fall in the north soon after midday. By 4 p.m., the sky over Kingstown was a pall of murky yellow, 'like the less noxious variety of yellow London fog'. At about the same time, huge dense flows of hot rock and ash (the nuée ardentes) avalanched down the sides of the volcano, leaving deposits a metre thick across much of northern St Vincent. At least fifteen hundred people died in this activity, as the flows swept without warning across sugar cane plantations, and through villages. Despite the enormous damage that the eruption caused at the time, the residents of the island were quickly re-housed. The tropical climate meant that plants recovered very quickly, although this was practically the final straw for sugar cultivation on St Vincent. Today, vast coconut plantations grow out of the thick brown soil that is now all that is left of the 1902 ash.

There was another, and smaller, eruption in 1979. This time, the north of St Vincent was safely evacuated, and ash fell once more across Barbados.

There are several lessons that we can learn from St Vincent. To those living through an eruption the effects can seem like the end of

Mt. Pelée

the world. But this has happened repeatedly in the past, and the island has recovered rapidly each time. For Barbados, which would otherwise be a barren lump of limestone on the edge of the Atlantic, these occasional dustings of ash are good news, as they provide an excellent mineral supplement for the local soils.

Mt. Pelée Gully

CHAPTER ELEVEN

VOLCANIC ISLANDS AND RIDGES

Much of the Earth's volcanism occurs far away from the edges of the continents, and deep under the sea. The oceanic ridges are the unsung and unseen workhorses of the planet. Volcanoes at the ridges erupt many cubic kilometres of lava every year. As a result, about one percent of Earth's surface is covered with fresh basalt every two million years. The oceanic ridges are also places where heat and chemicals move between the outside and the inside of the Earth. Sea-water sinks deep into the ocean crust at ridges. This returns, three hundred degrees hotter and chemically changed, to the sea floor at bizarre deep-sea vents. These vents, known as black smokers, release vast quantities of hot, mineral rich water. This is an ideal environment for unique deep-sea life forms, such as giant tubeworms and clams. Minerals, including iron, copper and zinc sulphides, accumulate in huge quantities around black smokers.

Many isolated volcanic islands are scattered across the floor of the ocean, far from any plate boundaries. These islands, which sometimes form small clusters, like the Azores, or trails of increasingly old volcanoes, like the Hawaiian chain, form above hotspots in the mantle. Hotspots are just one part of the heaving mass of rock in the mantle. Small patches of mantle that are hotter than their surroundings will rise, because they are less dense than the rock around them. As these patches rise towards the surface they eventually start to melt. The melt escapes,

The volcanic Island of Santorini, Greece.

forcing its way through the plate above, to form the volcano at the surface.

HAWAII

Hawaii is the most active volcanic island in the world today. It is made up of four volcanoes, each of which is in a different part of its lifecycle, and each of which erupts basalt lava. The youngest, most vigorous stage of activity is shown by Kilauea. Kilauea is a shield that rises twelve hundred metres above sea-level and has been erupting for most of the time since 1896. Since January 1983, lava has been pouring out of a set of vents along the 'East rift zone'. At times this lava erupts vigorously,

as jets and fountains of red hot spray. Most of the time it has emerged as torrents of fast-moving lava, flowing down a series of channels to the Pacific Ocean.

Mauna Loa is a mature shield volcano that rises four kilometres above sea-level and more than eight kilometres above the sea-floor. Mauna Loa is probably coming towards the end of its life, in geological terms, but has still had more than a dozen episodes of activity in the past hundred years. Eventually, as the plate moves over the hotspot still further, Mauna Loa will die, while Kilauea will grow into a shield of the same size as present-day Mauna Loa. The two other

A spectacular explosion of lava in the Hawaiian Islands.

Hawaii

volcanoes on Hawaii, Mauna Kea and Hualalai, are already well into their retirement. They remain active, but without the vigour and intensity of their earlier years. Already a new vent, Loihi, is forming offshore from Kilauea. This vent is still deeply submerged, but it will only be a few thousand years before it builds up to the surface.

ICELAND

Iceland is a rare example of what happens when a hotspot coincides with a spreading ridge. Like Hawaii, Iceland's volcanoes are rather prolific. Unlike Hawaii, Iceland is dominated by a rift which is continually pulling apart. This means that Icelandic volcanoes tend to be cones, or lines of cones, rather than shields. Iceland's volcanoes are also a little more diverse, producing both eruptions

of basalt lava and explosive eruptions of rhyolite pumice.

Several of Iceland's past eruptions have achieved notoriety. The volcano Hekla, in southern Iceland, has exploded violently several times in the last seven thousand years. Volcanic ash from each of these events can be found across northern Europe, trapped in peat bogs and archaeological sites.

The eruption at Laki in 1783 was the largest single eruption of lava in the last three hundred years. Over the space of eight months, about fifteen cubic kilometres of basalt sprayed out from a line of vents along a fissure. Flows of lava spilled across more than five hundred square kilometres of surrounding land. Gases from the volcano formed a noxious 'dry fog' that blanketed much of

*Laki Fissure,
Iceland*

Iceland, and drifted across northern Europe. This dry fog was a mixture of carbon dioxide and sulphuric acid, mixed with smaller amounts of hydrofluoric and hydrochloric acids. As well as its wider effects on the world's weather, these toxic gases had some awful effects on Iceland. Tens of thousands of cattle and horses and nearly two hundred thousand sheep died as a result, either through inhalation of poison gases, or lack of food, as the vegetation was destroyed. One fifth of the human population also died as a

Spectacular explosive eruption at HeimayIceland

consequence.

A more recent eruption from the Grimsvötn volcano had less devastating, but equally dramatic effects. Grimsvötn is a ten-kilometre wide, water-filled crater underneath Vatnajökull, the largest ice-cap in Iceland. On September 29, 1996, a magnitude 5 earthquake marked the start of an intense earthquake swarm. Within two days, an eruption started fifteen kilometres north of Grimsvötn. This eruption was a simple fissure-fed eruption of lava, underneath half a

kilometre of ice. As the lava came into contact with the ice, the magma froze and the ice melted. The result was a violent eruption that sent plumes of steam and ash rising three kilometres above the ice-cap. Along six kilometres of fissure, fire-fountains rapidly built up a blocky deposit of lava under the ice. The eruption continued for thirteen days before coming to a halt. Meltwater produced by the eruption flowed under the ice into Grimsvötn lake, raising the ice-cap as it did so. At the same time, the warm water started to melt its way through the ice-dam that corked the lake. Late on November 4th, five weeks after the eruption started, tremors from Grimsvötn warned that the ice-dam was giving way. Eleven hours later, the first trickle of sulphurous meltwater reached the edge of the ice-cap, fifty kilometres away from Grimsvötn . The trickle quickly turned into a flood of colossal proportions. Three cubic kilometres of meltwater raced out at up to

fifty thousand cubic metres per second, a flood rate that would put the Mississippi to shame. This dam-burst, or jökulhlaup, was one of the largest this century from Grimsvötn. In the rush of water, bridges and roads were swept away. As the water drained out from under the ice-sheet the ice and water pressure at the vent fell. A twenty-minute burst of ash marked the end of the eruption.

THE AZORES

The islands of the Azores are a final example of hotspot volcanoes. This group of seven islands remains very active, with some dramatic eruptions during the past three hundred years. The pleasantly mild and damp climate means that even the youngest deposits on land are overgrown. This gives a very misleading impression of the gentle nature of the islands. Sâo Miguel, the largest of the Azores, is home to three impressive

Agua de Pau, Azores.

Ancient pyroclastic flow deposits, Sao Miguel.

Many passing seafarers have described eruptions from the nearby submarine banks. Captain Tillard described one such in June 1811.

'We observed rising in the horizon two or three columns of smoke such as would have been occasioned by an action between two ships.'

As they approached closer, he continued,

'..the volcano burst upon our view in the most terrific and awful grandeur. Imagine an immense body of smoke rising from the sea. In a quiescent state it had the appearance of a circular cloud revolving on the water .. when suddenly a column of the blackest cinders, ashes and stones would shoot up in form of a spire. This was rapidly succeeded by a second, a third and fourth. The most vivid flashes of lightning continually issued from the blackest part of the cloud.'

An island rapidly built out of the sea while the eruption continued. Captain Tillard took the opportunity to land. Although the ash was 'too hot to allow our proceeding', Tillard found time to plant the Union flag and name the island 'Sabrina', after his boat, before leaving.

calderas. Each was formed by repeated explosive eruptions of silica-rich magma, and each will probably erupt again.

In 1808, a small eruption on Sâo Jorge produced a nuée ardente that was described vividly by a local priest, Father da Silveira.

'A typhoon of fire emerged from the volcano .. forming a powerful burning cloud that advanced as far as the church, burning more than thirty people. Some were so blistered and blackened that they were unrecognisable. The burning clouds were laden with dust which weighed them down and made them crawl along the ground. The entry of the slightest parts of these clouds into the lungs brought death.'

CHAPTER TWELVE

VOLCANOES IN THE SOLAR SYSTEM

Volcanoes can be found throughout the solar system. Some of these volcanoes would look familiar, if only we could visit them. Others have no parallel on Earth. Mercury, Mars, Venus and the Moon are all made of the same materials as Earth, predominantly silicon, iron and magnesium. The melting that occurs within these planets makes lavas like basalt. Further out in the solar system, the planets and their moons are made of frozen ices of water, ammonia or even nitrogen. Many of these bodies may well have melted in the past. The lavas on these are like icy cold slurries, and their eruptions are like spouting geysers rather than fountains of fire.

THE MOON

The Moon is now cold and quiet. Because it is so small, it lost its heat very quickly, and its volcanoes were only active in the distant past when it was still young and hot. Like Earth, most of the melts on the moon were types of basalt. The Moon has much lower gravity than Earth and no atmosphere, so its eruptions would have been spectacular. As the magma rose towards the surface, bubbles of gas

View of the full moon, showing its dark 'seas' and the two bright craters Tycho (near bottom) and Copernicus (north of Tycho)

would have started to form, as on Earth. But even the tiniest bubbles would have expanded to fill a huge space because of the low pressure at the surface. Even the smallest amount of gas in the melt would have caused a violent eruption. All lava eruptions on the moon would have started as fire-fountains. The lower gravity of the moon would have

Viking 1 spacecraft photograph of Mars showing the giant Olympus mons volcano at top right and the 3 volcanoes forming the Tharsis Mountains at centre right.

allowed these fountains to reach a much greater size than on Earth. The dark blotches that we can see on the face of the moon are the 'lunar maria'. These are seas of lava, that filled up from spraying vents and fissures. During vigorous fire-fountaining, the droplets of lava would still have been hot enough to flow once they had landed, and the sprays of molten rock would have turned into snaking torrents of lava. These eruptions would have been like huge fountains of water cascading into a pond.

Like the Earth's ancient komatiites, some of the moon's lavas were erupted at a temperature hot enough to melt their way into deep channels as they flowed across the surface. The long, winding 'rilles' that cut across the moon's surface are certainly old lava channels. If they were formed by melting, they must have been made by very vigorous and long-lasting eruptions.

MARS

Mars is another venerable planet that hasn't erupted for millions of years. It is covered with a single thick plate, so there are no chains of volcanoes around the plate edges as on Earth. The few volcanoes that remain on Mars

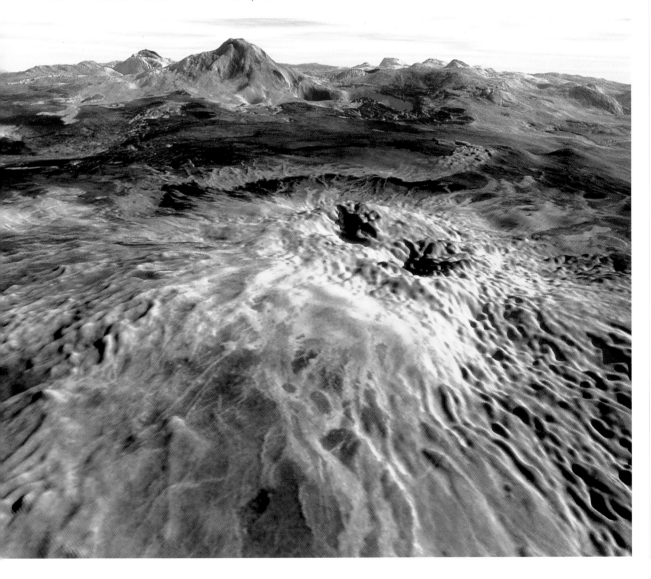

Computer-generated perspective of Sapas Mons, a large volcano on Venus. The summit is the bright feature in the foreground.

formed above hotspots, but are long since dead. The most enormous of these, Olympus Mons, rises twenty five kilometres above the surrounding plains, and is capped with a sixty kilometre wide crater. This is three times the height, and thirty times the volume, of Hawaii. Olympus Mons was able to grow so big for two reasons. Firstly, the plate that it sits on is static - it does not move away from the hotspot as our plates move on Earth. Secondly the plate on Mars is thicker and stronger than our tectonic plates. If Olympus Mons were on Earth, the plates would sag so much under the weight that it would not be able to survive.

Mars also has some huge plains covered with lava and pyroclastic flow deposits. On Earth, the biggest lava plains form where hotspots arrive under the continents. The largest of these, like the Deccan traps in India, or the Karroo basalts in South Africa, cover up to half a million square kilometres with one or two million cubic kilometres of lava. Alba Patera is the largest field on Mars. It covers over a million square kilometres with many millions of cubic kilometres of rock, and forms a huge flat-lying plain. The eruptions that made Alba Patera needn't have been any more vigorous than eruptions on Earth. They just lasted an awful lot longer.

VENUS

Of all the planets in the solar system, Venus is the most similar to Earth. It is just a little smaller than Earth, and has more or less the same composition. In other ways it is really very different. Venus is a planet with a 'runaway Greenhouse effect'. The atmosphere is a choking mixture of carbon dioxide gas and clouds of sulphuric acid. The pressure at the surface is the same as that at a depth of fifty to a hundred metres under water, while the temperature is high enough to melt lead. Since NASA's Magellan mission to Venus in the early 1990's, Venus has actually been mapped in more detail than our own planet. The depth of the oceans, combined with military secrecy have held back the mapping of Earth. What the NASA scientists found was extraordinary. Venus is covered with volcanoes, many of which are enormous structures, much larger than those found on Earth.

There are two interesting differences between Venus and Earth. The Magellan mission found no erupting volcanoes. This was unexpected since, if Venus is losing heat in the same way as Earth, it should be erupting tens of cubic kilometres of lava per year. Secondly, the mission found no evidence

False-colour image of tectonic ridge structures on the surface of Venus, made by the Magellan radar-mapping spacecraft in November 1990.

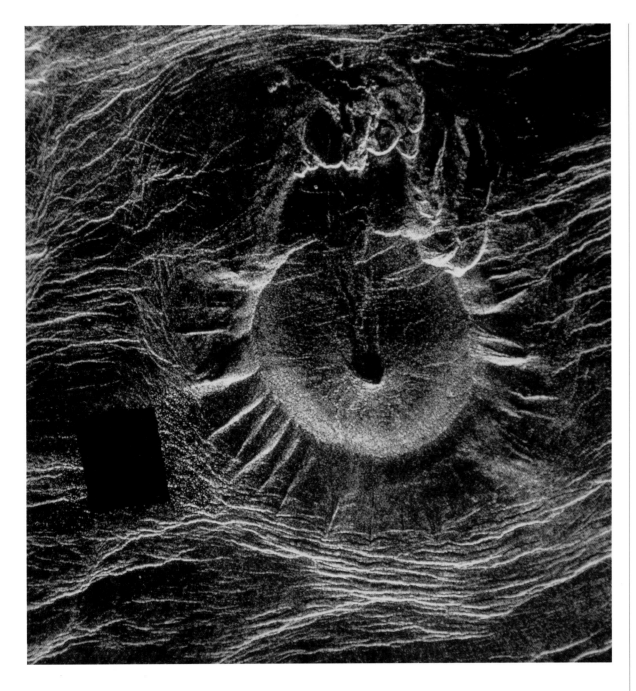

False-colour image of a volcanic edifice, measuring 35km in diameter at the summit, on Venus.

of tectonic plates like those on the Earth. Like Mars, much of Venus is covered by a single plate. Unlike Mars, though, this plate is young, and torn, or tearing, in places. Most volcanism is due to hotspots in the mantle, rather than due to activity at the edges of the plate. One theory suggests that the plate on Venus survives for about half a billion years, before sinking catastrophically in a flood of volcanism. Then the process begins all over again. Radar images of the surface show a bewildering array of different kinds of volcanoes that have formed above Venus's hotspots. In some places, clusters of small cones stretch across fields several hundred kilometres wide, just like smaller cone fields on Earth.

'Arachnoids' are circular structures criss-crossed with a spider's web of fractures. These have no parallel on Earth, and are

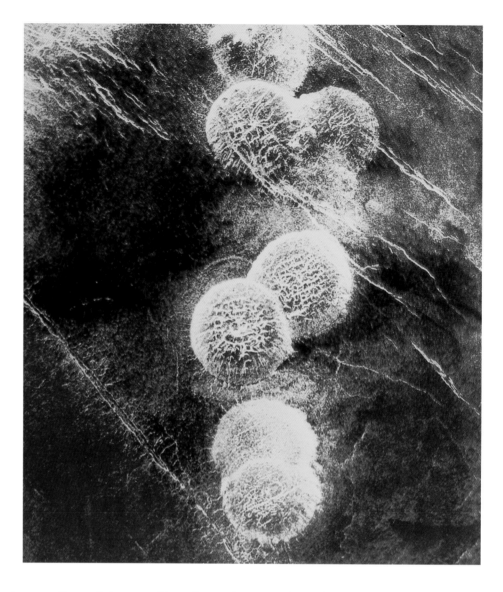

False-colour radar image of the Alpha Regio region of Venus. The seven dome-like hills are thought to have been created by successive lava eruptions.

perhaps huge collapsed domes of lava. Several hundred arachnoids have been found, each of which is up to a couple of hundred kilometres across. Larger still are 'coronae'. These enormous circular structures can be as large as a thousand kilometres across, and are usually associated with smaller volcanoes and lava flows. Coronae may form as huge bulges over the top of a rising hotspot, which then collapse after the hotspot dies.

Some of the most remarkable small volcanoes on Venus are domes. Domes on Earth are usually small; less than a few kilometres across. Domes on Venus are considerably larger; as much as fifty kilometres across. The difference may be due to the higher surface pressure on Venus. This means that Venus should have fewer explosive eruptions than Earth, and more large eruptions of lava. One group of domes, 'pancake' domes, are only a few hundred metres thick but spread, like pancakes, for tens of kilometres. Another set of domes have scalloped or fractured edges and reminded NASA scientists of huge ticks and anemones.

Venus also has some giant lava flow fields, and long, winding lava channels. The most extraordinary channels are a couple of

Computer-generated perspective of Maat Mons, the largest shield volcano on Venus.

kilometres wide and stretch for up to seven thousand kilometres. The longest lava flows on Earth rarely approach a hundred kilometres. How such long channels formed is perplexing. If they formed like lava channels on Earth, then the lavas must have been very hot, very fluid and have erupted at an enormous rate.

Io

Io is one of the most fantastic bodies in the solar system. It was discovered by Galileo Galilei over three hundred years ago, but it wasn't until 1979 that it was found to be volcanically active. Io is just a bit larger than the Moon, but it erupts more lava every day than the Earth. Its young surface is a multi-coloured patchwork of yellows, browns and reds, because it is covered with sulphur. Because it is so small and so far from the Sun, Io should be stone cold, and indeed, the surface temperature is one hundred and forty degrees below zero. But from Earth, infra-red telescopes can see warm spots, basking at twenty-five Celsius. The reason Io isn't frozen throughout is because it is trapped in an orbit

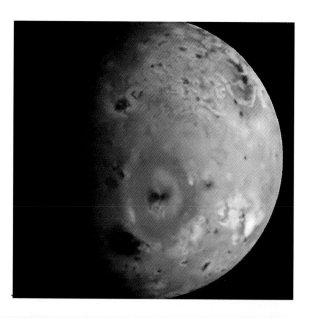

Enhanced-colour view of Io taken by the Galileo space-craft in June 1996. The prominent heart shaped feature surrounds a massive volcano called Pele.

that brings it within the reach of gravitational effects from Jupiter and its other moons. Huge tides push and pull the interior of Io around so that, like a squash ball, it eventually heats up. Except that on Io, temperatures get so hot that parts of it begin to melt. Inside Io, the magma is probably something like basalt. Yet the surface is covered with flows of sulphur. On Io the sulphur is something like the water on Earth. It is concentrated near the surface, is easily melted by heat from underneath, and is usually thrown out during eruptions.

Coloured Galileo spacecraft image of Io. The dark areas correspond to volcanic hot spots.

Voyager 1 photograph of an enormous volcanic eruption silhouetted against the blackness of space on Io.

The dozens of volcanoes on Io are incredibly active, each erupting at something like the rate of Hawaii. Because the atmosphere is almost non-existent, eruptions produce violent sprays of molten lava. These form huge umbrella-shaped fountains that rise four hundred kilometres from the surface of Io, and stretch for a thousand kilometres across. The largest fountains on Earth are a thousand times smaller than this.

The largest volcano on Io is called Pele. (All of Io's features are named after gods or heroes associated with fire, sun, thunder or volcanoes). Pele was first seen throwing out a three hundred kilometre high umbrella-shaped plume in 1979. It has erupted continuously since then. Pele has a reddish ring of deposits around it that is a thousand kilometres across, and which still continues to extend.

The aftermath of a recent eruption on Io was spotted in September 1997 during the Galileo satellite mission. Between April and September 1997, an eruption of the volcano Pillan Patera threw out a vigorous plume that reached over a hundred kilometres above the surface. An area four hundred kilometres across, the size of the state of Arizona, was covered with fresh, dark material.

EUROPA

Europa is another of Jupiter's four satellites that was discovered by Galileo Galilei in 1610. Europa is just a little larger than the Moon, but is many times brighter. It is covered in a surface of water-ice, that is frozen hard, but which shows a remarkably rough and varied surface texture. It is very likely that there is a deep ocean of liquid water beneath the surface. This layer of water is weak, and allows the ice crust to move around, like Earth's plates move around above the weak mantle. Where the ice crust pulls apart, water from the deep ocean rises up and freezes to make new crust. All of this can only happen because Europa is caught in the same orbital tug-of-war as Io, so that its deep ice and rock

mantle is continually squeezed and kept warm.

TRITON

Triton is a huge, frozen satellite of Neptune, which was imaged by the Voyager 2 mission, in 1989. The surface of Triton is so cold, just a few tens of degrees above absolute zero, that it is coated with frozen deposits of nitrogen and methane. There are very few impact craters on Triton's surface, so it must be young. Volcanism is the one way that the surface can be renewed. The images from the Voyager mission show tantalising evidence of active volcanism, or geysering. Two dark plumes rise eight kilometres from the icy surface, feeding long dark tails across one hundred and fifty kilometres. Perhaps these geysers are just surface features, formed by the heating of the icy layers by the distant sun. Or perhaps there is some deeper source of heat and molten material feeding the geysers.

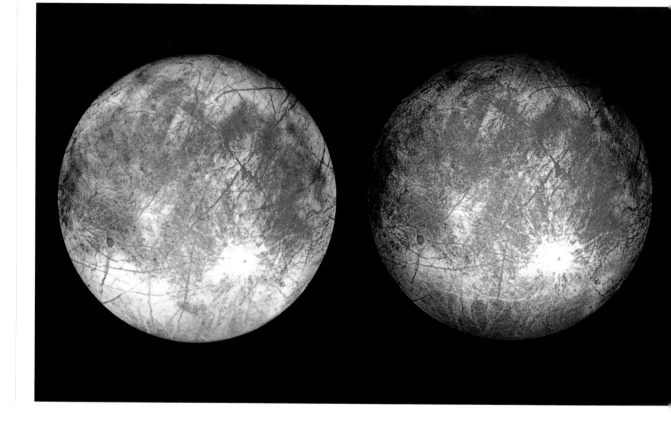

Two Galileo spacecraft images of Europa. The colour enhanced picture on the right shows the surface structure. Brown represents ice containing rock material, dark blue shows coarse-grained ice and light blue represents fine-grained ice.

Either way, Triton shows that even at the coldest and most distant fringes of the solar system, icy volcanoes play their part in shaping the surfaces of the planets and moons.

Colour-enhanced Voyager 2 image of Triton. The large polar cap which fills most of the picture is thought to consist of a slowly-evaporating layer of nitrogen.

CHAPTER THIRTEEN

PERILS AND PROTECTION

People will always want to live around volcanoes. From fertile soils to rich natural resources, the benefits outweigh the costs at least as long as the volcano slumbers. Millions of people live on or near volcanoes that have shown no sign of activity for hundreds of years. Most volcanoes erupt so infrequently that the risks of living next door are so slight as to be ignored. However, those unfortunate enough to live near a volcano when it erupts can face a high risk, if not of dying, at least of losing their homes or livelihoods.

Not all volcanoes are dangerous, and not all eruptions have the same effects, but the principal perils that volcanoes threaten us with are quite well known.

False-colour Landsat image of the eruption of Augustine volcano, Alaska

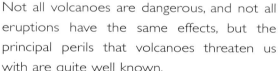

PYROCLASTIC FLOWS

Pyroclastic flows are the main killers. These flows are hot avalanches of rock, pumice and ash. They can fall from the side of a volcanic dome, as in Montserrat in the Caribbean, or cascade from a rising plume of ash and pumice. Either way, the effects are the same. Pyroclastic flows can move at hundreds of kilometres per hour, and can run out tens of kilometres from the volcano in large

eruptions. Flows usually follow valleys, but they can also climb small cliffs and hills and spread across the countryside. Few people have been hit by a dense flow and survived.

However, it is possible to be overrun by the ash clouds that accompany the flows, and live to tell the tale. At Mount St Helens, in 1980, and Montserrat in 1997 and elsewhere, people have survived by racing away from the flows in their cars, or by taking shelter. Some casualties from flows may be preventable. Flows kill for three reasons. They are hot, and cause severe burns. They are full of fine ash powder, that can choke. And they carry blocks of rock that can cause serious injury. By wearing plenty of clothing, sheltering inside strong, fire-resistant buildings, and breathing through a cloth, a person who was otherwise unable to escape a flow might still survive.

LAHARS

Lahars and mudflows are major hazards at all volcanoes that produce ash. From Sakurajima, in Japan, which continually drops ash onto its unstable slopes, to Pinatubo, the dangers from lahars can continue long after an eruption has finished. Lahars are usually only triggered by heavy rain storms. Light rain simply soaks in or runs off. Lahars can leave deposits metres thick, and as hard as cement, across huge

Part of the Alaskan coast seen from space.

Garage and car overwhelmed by ash, Montserrat, 1997.

areas away from the volcano. Bridges and houses can rarely withstand the force of a lahar, being swept away like toys in the raging torrent.

Little can be done to reduce the impact of lahars, without a massive investment of effort. Attempts were made on Pinatubo to build earth banks to divert the lahars. Few, if any, of these were successful, since they were unable to cope with the enormity of the flows. In Japan, 'sabo works' are used to protect against lahars. Deep and wide concrete channels direct the flows out to sea, preventing all but the largest lahars from spilling out uncontrollably.

Ash

Ash is one of the most widespread volcanic products. Almost all volcanoes produce ash and, because it is so fine, it can be carried for hundreds or thousands of kilometres by winds. Fresh ash deposits look deceptively like snow. It doesn't melt, though, and is much heavier. Twenty centimetres of ash is usually enough to collapse roofs. Far away from the volcano, even small amounts of ash are enough to damage engines, knock out computers and bring on asthma attacks.

Some volcanoes produce ash that is so fine that it can be inhaled. Exposure to fine ash for many years may bring on serious illnesses, like silicosis. Ash does have its uses though, in ceramics and building materials. Ash from Santorini, in Greece, was used in the building of the Suez canal, and is still used as a local building material.

Volcanic bombs

Even tiny steam explosions can hurl blocks of rock for hundreds of metres, or even

*Lava flow advancing
on Zafferana, 1992.*

kilometres. These explosions usually occur without warning. Safety equipment, such as hard hats, could have saved many of the tens of people killed by falling blocks in the last twenty years.

There are several effects of being hit by volcanic bombs. Hot blocks, too small to break bones or fracture skulls, can still cause severe effects in the wrong circumstances. A group of climbers filming an eruption of Popocatepetl, Mexico, died when they were caught in a shower of hot blocks near the summit. Most died because the blocks melted their synthetic clothes and stuck themselves to the climbers' skin causing massive burns. A layer of flameproof clothing would prevent a repeat of this and similar tragedies.

LAVA FLOWS

Lava flows usually damage little other than the buildings and land that happen to be in the way. The eruption of Nyiragongo in 1977,

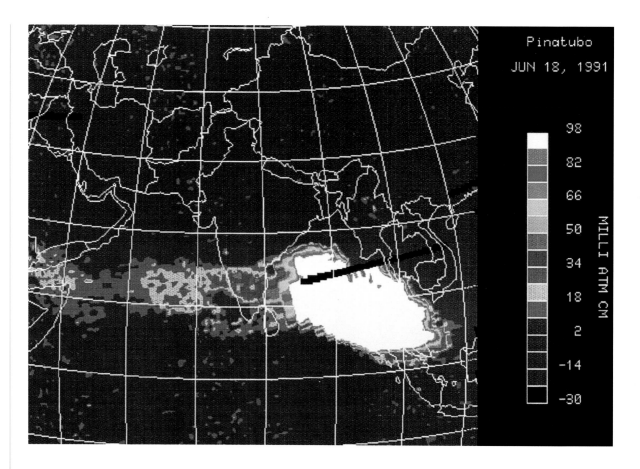

Pinatubo
JUN 18, 1991

98
82
66
50
34
18
2
-14
-30

MILLI ATM CM

False-colour map of sulphur-dioxide released by the Mt Pinatubo eruption in June 1991. The highest concentrations are shown in white.

where people were outrun by the flow of lava, was extremely unusual. Even in tropical climates, lava flows take many years to rot. On the Javan volcano of Lamongan, a few small trees grow on lava flows that are one hundred years old. Flows two hundred years old are home for banana trees, and flows three hundred years old are thickly forested. In arid environments, lava flows tens of thousands of years old can look like they erupted yesterday.

GASES

All volcanoes release gases into the air. Mostly these gases are steam and carbon dioxide, and are usually harmless. Carbon dioxide can be a problem if it becomes trapped. Since carbon dioxide is denser than air, it can collect in hollows. Every year people suffocate on volcanoes, by sleeping in old craters or vents. Lake Nyos, in the Cameroon, was a more

tragic example where carbon dioxide built up in the lake, before escaping as a suffocating blanket of gas.

Toxic gases can be a great problem. Fluorine and chlorine are usually present in volcanic gases. Fluorine is thought to have caused widespread deaths of livestock during the Laki eruption, Iceland, in 1783, with severe knock-on consequences for the people of the island. Fluorine-coated grass also led to sheep and cattle deaths after the small eruption of Cerro Hudson in Chile in 1995. Similar effects followed the 1995-6 eruptions of Ruapehu crater lake, New Zealand. These chemicals and others, such as sulphuric acid, take their toll on the plant life around volcanoes. Trees and shrubs that are downwind from a venting, steaming volcano will soon turn into gaunt, lifeless sticks.

TSUNAMI

Large eruptions at or below sea-level will often be followed by tsunami, often mistakenly called 'tidal waves'. There is nothing tidal about these waves. The usual cause of the wave is the force of the explosion. The Krakatau eruption in 1883 set off tsunami that were detected across much of the globe, although the effects were only severe within a few hundred kilometres of the volcano.

Tsunami can also be triggered by large landslides of material into the sea. One small tsunami formed after a few tens of millions of cubic metres of rock collapsed into the sea at Montserrat in December 1997. This had a peak wave height of only about a metre, and expired very quickly away from the island.

LARGE-SCALE LANDSLIDES

Recent images of the sea-floor offshore from the Hawaiian islands has shown that spectacular landslides can happen at volcanoes. Volcanoes are an unstable mixture of layers of hard rocks and soft rocks, and most grow relatively quickly. Many are also soaked through by hot, acidic groundwater that rots the volcanoes from the inside out. The result is that volcanoes become unstable as they become old, and some collapse as a result. One event, at Bandai-san in Japan in July 1888 swept an avalanche of one and a half cubic kilometres of mountainside across an area of over thirty square kilometres. A similar event happened during the Mount St Helens eruption in 1980.

Complete devastation of the forest caused by the Mt St Helens eruption, May 1980.

Deposits of the St Helens eruption 5 kilometres from the summit and deposited within minutes.

OTHER EFFECTS

Volcanic eruptions can also have local, regional and global effects on the weather or climate. In the past this has caused widespread food shortages and starvation. On the plus side, volcanic eruptions are one of the few ways of causing global cooling. The largest eruptions of the past twenty years have slightly checked the temperature rises seen as a result of global warming. The eruption of Pinatubo in 1991 happened in the right place and time to delay the start of that year's El Nino in the Pacific ocean, and may also have reduced its subsequent effects. Counteracting the effects of volcanic eruptions

There have been immense events at some of the Earth's largest volcanoes in the distant past. The giant landslide off Oahu covers twenty-three thousand square kilometres, and, in places, is over a kilometre thick. Fortunately these catastrophically large events are also very rare.

HAZARD MAPS

By studying past volcanic eruptions and their effects, and developing a picture of future eruptions at any specific volcano, it is possible to produce a hazard map. The simplest hazard map shows which valleys are likely to fill with

Ancient rice fields buried by a volcanic eruption of Asoma, Japan

pyroclastic flows and lahars, which areas will suffer from falling rocks, and which others may be covered by ash. In most short eruptions there may be little time for the geologists to produce a hazard map. The aim in these eruptions will usually be to work out the likely 'worst case scenario' and advise the authorities accordingly. One example of a hazard map that was tragically prophetic, but which was not implemented in time, was that produced at Nevado del Ruiz in Colombia in 1985. Here the mudflows followed exactly the path expected, and wiped out the town of Armero on their way.

A more successful hazard map was produced at Pinatubo in 1991, which led to the successful and safe evacuation of many people from the danger zone.

Hazard maps on Montserrat have evolved as the eruption continues. Early on, the danger zone was quite small, but as the dome grew larger, so did the exclusion zone. By mid-1997 the exclusion zone had extended to cover almost two-thirds of the island. So far, nearly all of the areas expected to be affected by pyroclastic flows have been, and those that remain untouched may not remain so for long.

INTERVENTION

It is always tempting to wonder whether human intervention could reduce the effects of an eruption, by diverting flows or blasting domes apart. For most eruptions however, even the most strenuous of efforts would be pathetic compared to the enormous natural power of the volcano, and is simply not worth contemplating. There are, though, a few examples of small eruptions of lava, where flows have been slowed or diverted. The first

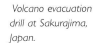

Volcano evacuation drill at Sakurajima, Japan.

serious efforts were in 1669, on Etna, when the inhabitants of Catania attempted to divert the flow around the city by setting to with pick-axes, and building stone walls. The attempts failed, partly because of the protestations of the villagers who stood to lose out if the flow was diverted. There have been continued efforts since then. During the 1992-3 eruption, earth banks tens of metres high and hundreds of metres long delayed the advance of the lava down the Val Calanna towards Zafferana. Diversion further down the volcano was not practical, as the path of the diverted flows would still cause damage to other land, roads and houses. Attempts to block Etna's lava tubes in 1992 were less than successful, as the concrete blocks that were dropped onto the lava from helicopters failed to sink. A final attempt to divert the main lava

Montserrat's East Coast, overrun by pyroclastic flows, 1997.

channel by excavation and explosion was eventually successful.

Dykes and dams have been used on Hawaii at times since 1955 to divert flows around key buildings. While this was successful for the thin, fluid pahoehoe flows, it was less so for thicker, blocky aa flows. In most cases, planning land usage around volcanoes is cheaper and more effective than building defences.

Another way to change the course of a lava flow is to cool it. This was first tried in Hawaii in the early 1960's, where the flows were slowed down by spraying water over the

advancing lava. This allowed just enough time for the residents of Kapoho to salvage some belongings before their houses succumbed. A more successful example was the 1973 eruption of Heimay, Iceland. Here the lava threatened one of Iceland's prime harbours. By pumping millions of tons of seawater onto the flow fronts, parts of the flows were stopped, and the harbour was saved.

EVACUATION

The eruption of Rabaul, Papua New Guinea, in 1995 shows the benefits of evacuation as protection against the effects of an eruption. The volcanic crisis in 1983-5 proved to be a useful practice for the later events of 1995. In 1984, there was an upsurge in the number of earthquakes around the volcano. Worried that this activity might mark the start of an explosive eruption, the authorities prepared for a major evacuation. Seismic activity decreased without warning, the threat of an

Bubbles of gas bursting in a lava pond, Oldoinyo Lengai, 1998.

eruption subsided, and an evacuation wasn't needed. Ten years later, the eruption of 1995 was preceded by just twenty-seven hours of earthquakes. Many of the residents of Rabaul remembered the events of 1984 and evacuated spontaneously. A huge loss of life was avoided as a result.

The risk with evacuations, though, is the danger of false alarms. The most celebrated example of this was in 1976 on the Caribbean island of Guadeloupe. Over seventy thousand people were evacuated as the Soufrière began to steam. Arguments between scientists and politicians caused turmoil, and the evacuation disintegrated. Steam explosions continued for nine months, and then petered out. No lives were lost, but the credibility of the decision-makers had been severely compromised.

Since 1986, six hundred thousand people have been evacuated from volcanoes that did eventually erupt. As a result, fewer than a thousand people died in these eruptions. While the social and economic costs of evacuation can be high, the benefits are obvious.

Mount Fuji, Japan.

CHAPTER FOURTEEN

PREDICTING THE FUTURE

Volcanologists study volcanoes for many reasons. Among the most important is the wish to foresee future activity. There are two slightly different ways of describing the future: forecasting and prediction. Forecasting is easy, but can be of little practical use. A forecast is simply a statement that future activity is expected within a certain period of time. Based on activity in the recent past we can forecast that there will be another small eruption of lava on Santorini, Greece, within the next century; or that there will be another eruption of Mauna Loa, on Hawaii,

within the next twenty years. With a bit of effort, we could also estimate the probability of these forecasts being correct. A prediction is a more specific description of what will happen, where and when. From current knowledge alone it is not possible to make any specific predictions about future activity at either Santorini or Mauna Loa.

Not all volcanoes behave predictably. A volcano can show one of a number of different patterns of behaviour. At some volcanoes eruptions occur randomly. Here,

Image derived from satellite radar information showing deformation of Mt Etna after eruption. Each cycle of red, yellow and purple fringes indicates a deflation of around 3cm.

we might be able to work out the chance that there will be an eruption next year. There will be the same chance of an eruption in ten years time, or in a hundred years. Other volcanoes erupt constant amounts of lava from one period to the next. At these volcanoes, the longer the delay between eruptions, the larger the next eruption will be. Finally, there are volcanoes where eruptions occur in clusters, with long periods of quiet in between. The challenge at these volcanoes is to spot the beginning, or end, of a cluster. Of course, all of this assumes that a volcano's future behaviour will be the same as it was in the past. Whatever the behaviour of the volcano, the only way to detect the start of a new eruption is to watch the volcano for unusual signs. Many eruptions are preceded by a few days, weeks or months of increasing activity. From earthquakes, through steam or gas emissions to bulges appearing on the

volcano, there are usually tell-tale signs before activity starts. If we could only read these signs, then prediction should be possible.

Being able to predict the climax of an eruption might not always be useful. Imagine the chaos, and potential for disaster, if we were only able to predict the start of an eruption within hours of the event. Cities near volcanoes would be seized by gridlock as people tried to flee. Fortunately, most volcanoes seem to take longer than just a few hours to warm up to a peak.

We are still far from being able to anticipate the start of activity at volcanoes that haven't erupted for years. As the eruptions of El Chichon, Mexico, in 1982, Pinatubo in 1991 and Montserrat in 1995 have all shown, it is not unusual for volcanoes to awake suddenly after many years asleep. However, as Pinatubo

View of the Montserrat lava dome, 1998.

Mapping a volcano. Oldoinyo Lengai, 1993.

showed, there may still be a long enough time between the start of activity and the eruption climax that it is possible to prepare for the event. It also helped that Pinatubo was well behaved, so that the forecasts of increasing activity proved correct throughout the crisis.

Long-lasting eruptions, or eruptions at well-studied volcanoes, give us the best

Satellite receiver used to measure the exact location of a point on the volcano.

chance of finding the key signs that warn of changes in activity. Volcanoes on Hawaii show some regular patterns before an eruption starts. At Mauna Loa, eruptions in 1975 and 1984 both started after a couple of years of increasing numbers of earthquakes close to the summit. These earthquakes showed that molten rock was pushing high up into the volcano, and breaking rock as it did so. At both Mauna Loa and Kilauea, the surface starts to deform as the volcano fills up with molten rock. This deformation can be detected with sensitive instruments on the volcano, or by measurements from satellites. The summit of the volcano rises slowly, perhaps a couple of metres. Then, just before the eruption starts, lava drains into the fracture system on the way to the vent. The surface drops rapidly as a result. Depending on how far the vent is from the centre of the volcano, changes in the

Installing monitoring equipment on the flanks of the volcano. Montserrat, March 1998.

height of the summit might happen before the lava bursts out at the surface. Unfortunately, the overflow valve at Kilauea isn't very well regulated, so it isn't yet possible to predict when an eruption will start just by seeing how far the summit has risen.

Montserrat's volcano shows many regular patterns of behaviour. At times when lava is erupting steadily, and the dome is growing, avalanches of rock occur regularly every eight to twelve hours. The starting and stopping of these regular cycles reflects changes in the underlying behaviour of the volcano. While we can recognise the start and end of the cycles, understanding what it all means remains the next problem to solve.

A loose analogy describes the current state of volcano prediction. Imagine reading a novel, starting from page one. Early on, as long as it is written in a language we can understand, it may be possible to recognise the genre, or perhaps even the author. This gives some clues as to how the novel will develop. If there are no chapter headings, could you spot when the next chapter was going to start before it arrived? Or would you even know when you

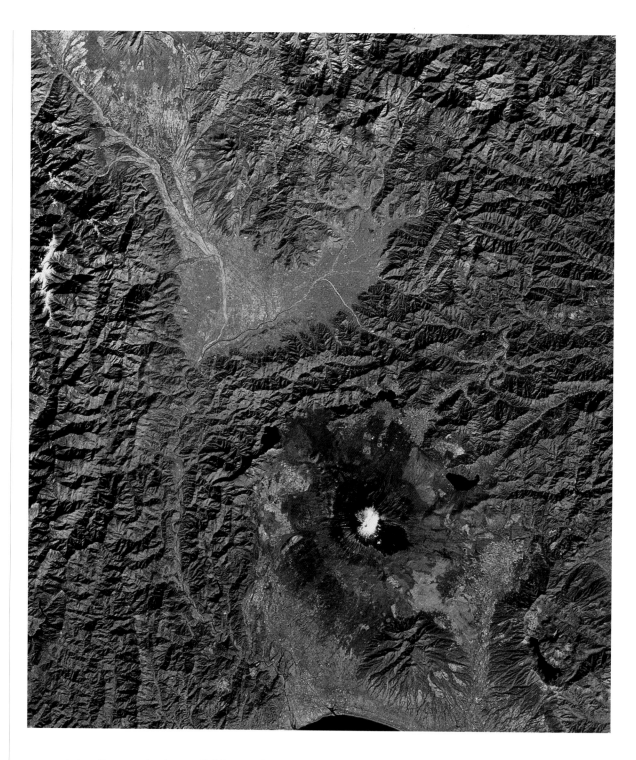

*Satellite image of
mt Fuji, Japan.*

were into the next chapter? Now take this one step further. As you progress through the book, the pages are handed to you one by one. Can you tell when the book might end? Perhaps there are signs that start to appear as the end approaches. Or we could assume how long a typical book is, and guess from

that. In the end, if we don't know whether or not the author likes to tie up the ends before finishing, or whether there is a dramatic finale ahead, we have to pore over what has passed in the hope that this will illuminate the future.

GLOSSARY

Aa - a type of lava flow with a rough, blocky surface.

Andesite - a type of volcanic rock. Andesite is intermediate in composition between basalt and dacite, and contains about 60 percent silica. Andesite is common in volcanoes above subduction zones.

Ash - any rock particles or crystals thrown out by volcanoes that are less than 2 mm in size.

Basalt - the most abundant volcanic rock on Earth. Basalt contains about 50 percent silica. Most basalt erupts to form black lava flows. Block and ash flow - one type of pyroclastic flow where the fragments carried by the flow are mostly dense blocks of lava.

Caldera - a large volcanic crater, usually formed by collapse of the volcano during large eruptions. Calderas can be kilometres or tens of kilometres across with steep cliffs up to a kilometre high.

Cinder cone (or scoria cone) - a steep conical hill formed during fire-fountaining, and usually made of frozen droplets ('cinders' or 'scoriae' of basalt or andesite).

Conduit - the pipe, crack or fracture through which magma flows.

Crust - the outermost layer of the Earth. The crust is between thirty and seventy kilometres thick on the continents, and six to eight kilometres thick under the oceans. Crust is usually cool or cold.

Dacite - a common volcanic rock that forms pumice, or glassy lava. Dacite contains about 65% silica. Dacite lava is very sticky, and often forms domes or stubby flows.

Dome - a steep-sided pile of lava formed by the eruption of sticky lava.

Dyke - a steep fracture filled with magma. Most magma rises through the outer layers of the Earth through dykes.

Feldspar - a white or colourless mineral that is found in many types of volcanic rock.

Fire fountain - an incandescent spray of red-hot droplets of melt. Fire fountains can reach several hundred metres high on Earth, and can stretch for kilometres along erupting fissures. Fire-fountaining is common at basaltic volcanoes.

Granite - a slowly cooled, light-coloured crystalline rock made up mainly of crystals of feldspar and quartz. Granite is the coarse-grained equivalent of volcanic rocks like dacite or rhyolite.

Hot spot volcano - an isolated volcano or group of volcanoes that forms above hot, upwelling part of the Earth's interior. Hot spot volcanoes need not lie near to the boundary between two tectonic plates.

Ignimbrite - a pumice-rich deposit formed by a pyroclastic flow.

Jîkulhlaup - an Icelandic term for a sudden burst of water that escapes from a glacier

Kimberlite - a rare volcanic rock-type that usually fills narrow, deep vents in areas of very old crust. Some kimberlites contain small amounts of diamond.

Komatiite - a rare form of basalt that contains about 40 percent silica. Komatiite was only common more than two billion years ago. Komatiite lava is hotter and more fluid than basalt.

Lahar - a volcanic 'mudflow'. Lahars are mixtures of ash and rock fragments in water, that flow with the consistency of wet cement, and may be hot.

Lava - molten rock that flows over the surface of a volcano as a very dense fluid and solidifies to form a hard, dense rock

Lithosphere - the rigid outer shell of the Earth. The lithosphere includes the crust and the coolest upper parts of the mantle.

Maar - a form of volcanic crater. Maars are often a few hundred metres wide, up to a hundred metres deep, and filled with water.

Magma - a general term that describes molten rock below the surface. Magma erupts either to form lava, or pyroclastic rock when it reaches the surface.

Mantle - the interior of the Earth that extends from the base of the crust to a depth of 2900 km. Below the lithosphere, the mantle is hot enough to flow.

Mudflow - a flowing slurry of water, rock and mud.

Nuée ardente - literally a 'glowing cloud'; a form of pyroclastic flow.

Obsidian - a black volcanic glass of rhyolite or dacite composition.

Olivine - a green mineral commonly found in basalt lava.

Pahoehoe - a type of lava flow with a smooth but ropy surface.

Phreatic eruption - steam-driven explosion of ash and rock.

Plinian eruption - an explosive eruption that forms a vertical column of ash and pumice which rises several tens of kilometres into the atmosphere.

Pumice - a volcanic rock that is so full of gas bubbles that it has a very low density. Pumice fragments can often float on water.

Pyroxene - a black coloured mineral common in basalt and andesite.

Pyroclastic flow - a hot avalanche of ash, rock and gas. Flows often have a thick, dense lower part underneath a billowing, more dilute cloud of ash and hot air

Pyroclastic rock - a general term for any volcanic material that is ejected as broken, solidified fragments of rock.

Rhyolite - a type of volcanic rock that commonly erupts as pumice. Rhyolite typically contains about 75 percent silica and is the stickiest lava known.

Rille - a type of long sinuous channel, found on the Moon.

Rift - the fracture system that forms where two tectonic plates pull apart (like the oceanic ridges) or where a single plate is being pulled apart (like the East African rift).

Scoria - dark-coloured droplets or fragments of basalt or andesite, typically formed during fire-fountaining

Stratocone - a volcanic cone built up of both pyroclastic deposits and lavas during more than one eruption. Stratocones are usually quite steep, and may be several kilometres high

Subduction zone - the place on Earth's surface where two tectonic plates converge, and one plate plunges into the mantle

Surge - pyroclastic surges, sometimes called 'base surges', are a violent form of pyroclastic flow. Surges move as ground-hugging dilute ash and gas flows. They are often wet or damp, and may be caused by eruptions through water.

Tectonic plate - the rigid, outer layer of the Earth is divided into several tectonic plates, each of which is about 100 km thick. Tectonic plates move apart at rifts, and converge at subduction zones.

Tephra - a general term used to describe any type of pyroclastic rock

Tsunami - a sea wave produced by an underwater earthquake or volcanic explosion.

Vent - the opening at the Earth's surface through which material erupts.

Viscosity - a measure of a liquid's resistance to flow, or its 'stickiness'. The most fluid basalt hasa viscosity similar to thick engine oil. Andesite lava can be several thousand times stickier than basalt; rhyolite is at least a million times more viscous.

INDEX

Picture Credits:

David Pyle

pp. 6, 8, 10, 12 (bottom), 23 (bottom), 24, 25, 26, 27, 33, 35 (bottom), 36, 38, 39, 44, 45, 49, 52, 53, 55, 65, 67, 68, 70, 71, 72, 81 (bottom), 82, 83, 84, 85, 90, 96, 110, 111, 113, 114, 115, 116, 119, 120, 121,

GeoScience Features Picture Library

pp. 2, 5, 29, 41, 43, 46, 47 (bottom), 48, 56/57, 59, 62/63, 64, 69, 73, 74, 75, 76, 77, 79, 80, 81 (top), 86, 87, 88, 89, 92, 93, 94, 95,

Science Photo Library Ltd

pp. 7, 9, 11, 12 (top), 13, 14, 15, 17, 18, 19 (top), 21, 22, 23 (top), 28, 30, 31, 34, 35 (top), 37, 40, 42, 47 (top), 50, 51, 54, 60, 66, 78, 91, 97, 98, 99, 100, 101, 102, 103, 104, 105, 106, 107, 108, 109, 112, 117, 118, 122,